THE KEYS TO BALANCE AND POWER

THE KEYS TO BALANCE AND POWER

Vincent Garcia

Drawings by D'Ali

Inspired by my Mother, Luciana

This was my personal experience. This is why I wrote this book. I lived through the process of success, failure, punishment and redemption into a new life.

It happened. Things happen. It is what it is. Whether "it" is that I was confined in a prison cell or whether "it" is that your significant other left you and you hurt in ways you couldn't imagine. You are, where you are. Yes, you are hurting and afraid, and you could be heading for a dark time. But how can you unfreeze and move forward? How can you gain from this? How can you harvest good from this trial and tribulation? How can you find the Treasure in Adversity?

Understand the situation and make a plan. Do not run from it. Face it. Take away its power. I know it can be done because I did it in the darkest of times.

I understood that being in prison would be difficult if I allowed it to be difficult. Because I knew it was inevitable, I decided that I would make myself immune to the feelings of despair, loneliness, abandonment, selfpity, regret, blame, self-doubt, suspicion, loss of control and generally all negative thoughts. I understood that I could gain power from the Adversity, or I could allow Adversity to weaken and defeat me. I understood that it was going to be difficult. I made a commitment to myself that I would not abandon myself, because that is all I had left..... myself.

I also knew that I was now in a place where I could grow physically, spiritually, emotionally and mentally, if I allowed the prison experience to teach me and temper me. I knew that if I harvested the opportunity (and yes, I did consider it an opportunity), I would grow in ways that only Adversity can teach and temper you. I knew that if my Mind was right, I would gain Peace, Purpose and Power. In fact, that is exactly what happened. The experience was transformed from Punishment to Power.

Contents

Contents

FOREWORD

Balance and Power. That has a nice sound to it. Somehow, they belong together. Everyone wants these strengths in their lives. They are indeed magical. I have learned that in order to have Power, you must first develop Balance, an even head and unflappable force of will and confidence; to have Balance you must have Discernment; to have Discernment you must have Awareness and to have Awareness you must have a Listening for it. To have Listening you must practice Listening. And when you have these strengths, you are indeed a very powerful person in this world. You may have known someone like this. You can feel their Power.

This book is intended to create a path for you to develop Balance and Power in your life. This world is a frenzied hot mess. Every day you feel like you are marching toward the jaws of the dragon; voluntarily. However, learning these disciplines requires sacrifice and practice for which many are unwilling to pay the price.

The word Power in this context is not meant to convey a meaning of physical or overbearing power, but instead a state of being; a state of mind, mindfulness and spirit that says that you have deep and spiritual personal power that guides and protects you on your daily path and makes you Undefeatable in the face of every single thing that you might encounter, whether it be ill health, broken finances, estrangement from loved ones, a failed marriage or any other event that we normally consider a failure or a negative event in our lives. Unfortunately, Power is easily abused and can be taken for granted. Our goal is to gain this Power and maintain the Balance needed to keep it pure and true through Purity of Intent.

I must confess, that I had an unfair advantage in developing Balance and Power. My friend and Mentor was Adversity. Adversity was my loyal companion on this path of learning.

My childhood was pretty brutal. Summers were spent working in the adobe fields from 4am until 9pm, Monday through Saturday. Many times, there was nothing to eat. With twelve mouths to feed, food was sometimes scarce. Going to school in old and worn clothes was the norm. But when things are so hard, when you eventually have something, you really appreciate it. Yes, I had the unfair advantage of struggle and Adversity. It teaches you in a manner that nothing else can. There is no substitute. Later in life, when I was convicted of a federal crime and spent two years in a federal prison, it was my childhood and the strength given and taught to me by my father and mother that prepared me for the challenges of prison.

As I wrote this book, I thought often of the many people who influenced my life and thinking in so many profound ways. I was indeed fortunate and blessed to have such a breadth of influence that gave me a varied platform from which to develop my own manner of thought. I continue to have many people in my life who share their deep and abiding ideas and thoughts with me on a daily basis. We don't always agree, but I listen attentively to them to gain their Perspective for how they see the world today and how they handle its myriad challenges. And there are many challenges in this troubled world. Just when it seems we have found the answers to some of life's questions, we learn once again that life and history are cyclical and that we should have learned, but didn't.

However, it is my intent and goal to focus not on the negative, the problems, the troubles and desperation that seem to fill our world today, but instead to study the many ways and avenues that we can seek, find and engage in order to make this world and our own individual worlds and universes, peaceful and fulfilled places. That is the reason for the word "challenge". It is something to meet and address; something that can be accomplished. You are not defeated; you are simply temporarily challenged for a greater purpose and far greater meaning.

I think often about my parents and how they influenced my life and thinking. My father was the strict Catholic disciplinarian, who worked the old-fashioned way. He was an artist who built custom adobe homes from the ground up. He made and harvested his own building materials. He made adobe bricks by hand, went to the mountains to cut and harvest "vigas", (the ponderosa pine beams used to support the roof) and did his own plastering, flooring and painting. He was up at four in the morning every day and worked sometimes until midnight by the light of his truck's headlights. He was from the school of thought that there was no single thing that could not be done. He was a hard and powerful man. But in the beginning and for years after, it was a humble living. I like to say in jest that I was raised in a mud hut, but that's really not true, but as soon as we could afford one, we did move into one. However, his efforts did eventually lead to financial success, and it was a hard earned, difficult path but he earned it the old-fashioned way.

Despite his toughness, he had this kind and gentle manner. When he was taking a short break to have a drink of water, or at day's end, he would physically stand back from his work and just look at it. He loved the natural features of the adobes and the grains of the wood beams. He took great care in his work and derived Power from it. Then, almost as if he was in love with his creation, he would walk up to a still raw section of wall he had just built and gently caress it with the palm of his hand while looking at it in the most intimate way.

It was an experience to behold. It was in every sense, a prayer to his Creator. His work had Purpose and it brought him Peace.

As a World War II veteran like many in his "great generation", he feared nothing. So, his life was full of dichotomies. He was a person of extremes. He never de-programmed from the war and still had to experience the thrill of battle in some way. He would get into a fight or negotiate a deal in hard ball style, then stop on his way and give an indigent $100.00 without need for a "thank you" and he would never tell anyone he did it. His generosity was a sight to behold and, in some ways, it was a conflicting message. Observing those acts created the beginnings of my personal journey to Balance and Power.

My mother was the only person on the planet who could have lived with my father. She had twelve children. It is hard to understand how one human being could have so much love and strength in her body and soul. Yet, she did. She too was from the old school of Catholic faith, marriage, children, forgiveness and reconciliation. I loved going to mass with her every morning during school. We lived close to San Felipe Catholic Church in Old Town; Albuquerque. I begged her to wake me up early so that I could go to the 6AM mass with her. I dressed hastily to not make her late. She wore a scarf on her head as was the custom then. I remember walking with her on cold mornings, hugging her bright red coat under her arm trying to keep myself warm, while at the same time wondering, "why did I want to do this"? She would walk playfully fast to make it clear she was kind of in a hurry too. Those are such rich and vivid memories for me. The colors, the cold, the feelings of closeness, my dependence on her, all wrapped into one glorious piece of life's art. It was bliss not knowing that we didn't have riches.

We had a humble living until all my father's hard work paid off. And my mother was right there with him, every laborious step of the way.

I remember we would stand in line at dinner time and my mother would serve us to make sure there was enough for everyone. There were no second servings and we learned to eat slowly and fully appreciate every bite of every meal. When times were harder, we would eat rice or beans almost every day. Some days the rice was different, for which I was immensely grateful. Many years later I realized she put food coloring in the rice each day to make it look different and more appealing. I now appreciate what she did to make us feel like we had variety. I think about that now and my heart clutches with the love and appreciation I feel for her. I imagine how she must have felt knowing what she was doing in her humble yet creative way to care for her children.

Yes, those were gratifying and fulfilling days even if we didn't know it then. There were simple rules and discipline, and the problems and troubles of the new age were not yet upon us.

It is difficult to arrive at the "here and now" and somehow handle all of what happens in this modern world of ours. I wonder, as do you, I'm sure, how this all happened. How on earth did we get here? (Not how did we get here on Earth. That's a different question for a different time.) Sometimes I wonder what "modern" really means and what it has done to us as feeling and thinking human beings. We get so numb to all that happens around us that we get far away from that which is really important. Sometimes I wonder what "Western Civilization" has done to our natural and spiritual world. Clearly there are many truly wonderful accomplishments in our modern society. By way of example, if one were to contemplate and study English Common Law and the new level of civility it engendered in our society, one would recognize that that one singular civil progression changed us and made us a better people. For its time and even today, if properly applied, it can be considered an enlightenment. A speedy trial, by a jury of your peers to name just two elements of those laws, changed everything from the unjust taking and holding of falsely accused persons for the sole benefit of the king, to the economics of the time. The changes to society were profound and helped us build a better society. However, as we fast forward to our current society and observe how those same laws have changed ostensibly for the better, we see an entirely different landscape. From the simple beginnings of human rights in the era of Hammurabi, who was the first to codify and publish a set of moral laws (including the 'lex talionis' or 'an eye for an eye'), to overwhelming rights pushed upon us today by a system of over 300,000 laws that purport to "protect" us, even from ourselves, is sometimes absurd. As malleable creatures we tend to Surrender to so-called protections, security and comforts at the expense of our self-reliance, self-responsibility and Personal Power. We are entitled to countless benefits bestowed upon us by a "compassionate" government. But we should not forget that everything has a price. We do so at our own peril.

There are myriad troubles in our world today. I don't need to recite them here, besides while you are reading this, something new will emerge on the global theatre. Today, it seems we are affected by events all over the globe. Consumption in China; labor in India; oil in the Mideast; global warming; climate change, viruses, immigration and everything else. In the past, events and issues were more local and therefore life seemed simpler. The past it seems, was a far simpler time to be alive. But only in some ways. Who among us would gleefully trade our homes and comforts of today for those hardships of yesterday? None or few, I suppose. There are not many Mother Teresa's among us, and in a way, that is as it should be. Have you ever asked yourself "could I do what she did"? "Could I *really* do that"? If you have, your answer was probably "yes, I would want to if I wasn't married, if I didn't have children, if I wasn't in college, if I was younger, if I was older, if I was in better health, if I had money to pay my bills while I was gone".... Ad infinitum.

Conditions are seldom perfect for success

So, what is the purpose of gaining Balance and Power in today's world? Why should we care? Why not just Surrender? It is because we can live this "once in this Eterniverse" life and make it a special, purposeful and enlightened experience. We can engage and disengage as the occasion may require. Listen and Inquire at the appropriate times. We can become instruments of Patience, Strength, Peace, Gratitude, Forgiveness, Reconciliation, Redemption and Sharing. This is our singular and unique contribution to the Eterniverse from this place. No one else can do exactly what you can do. No one. This is your time. This is your space. Learn to gain your unique Balance and Power and live your own balanced and powerful life.

In writing this book, it has been my desire to simply discuss some of the thoughts and questions that I have had over my lifetime; thoughts that made me wonder about the underlying truths and reality that really govern our lives even though we are unaware of or simply don't think about them on a constant basis. It is my desire to share ideas with you that perhaps you have also had but have never discussed with anyone for fear that you would be considered a heretic or an unbeliever. Together we dare to inquire; to ask the hard questions knowing there may be no answers.

These writings represent a message and discussion from a very personal standpoint; from my heart and soul to your heart and soul. There is no judgment of anyone, and all thoughts and opinions are not only welcome but necessary. However, I am fully aware that some of the concepts discussed here will raise eyebrows if not ire from those who adhere to a more fundamental philosophy. Some of these discussions may be uncomfortable and disconcerting to some readers. Notwithstanding, it is my heartfelt hope that we open our minds and spirits to a new "Tao", a path that leads to Balance and Power in our lives.

As I wrote these words and expressed my thoughts, I experienced the most difficult personal time in my life. I got divorced, became estranged from my children, closed my company and several real estate and business developments, lost everything I had worked for over four decades and served two years in a Federal prison after being charged with federal white-collar crimes. These experiences have been a real-life test of the ideas and principles discussed in this book. They have presented me with an opportunity of a lifetime to experience these things and to rely on my own writings and thoughts to travel through this path and develop and maintain my own Balance and Power. Countless revelations have surfaced of which the most important are those that brought understanding in the most profound way. For this, I am grateful. The price paid is immeasurable, but the catharsis, personal growth and understanding and its application to my new path is equal. I am traveling through and authoring my Book of Life in all its uniqueness, just as you are. My life would not be complete without having had that experience.

This is my hope. that the thoughts in this book will serve as a guide for you in your "Book of Life". That you can remember just one thought or writing to apply to any situation that arises in your path. That you will become fulfilled and challenged by these writings.

That you will stop and think. That you will find your own special Balance and Power. That your enlightenment in this time and space will transcend seamlessly into the next existence, whatever you believe that to be.

Vincent

The keys to

Balance and Power

In a Frenzied World

The Fruit of Noble Struggles is a Glorious one
(from the Book of Wisdom)

We live in a very unique and special time in the history of humanity, and our place in the world and in the Eterniverse. Sometimes it is exciting, sometimes it is interesting and often it is frightening and threatening. As far as we know and are aware of the Eterniverse of things, this is a first for so many things in the world, as we know it. Things change from one moment to the next. Nothing seems certain. Today the rule is "expect the unexpected." On the surface, everything seems normal. Look out at the city lights from an elevated vantage point or out the window of an airplane. Everything looks calm and peaceful much like looking at the stars in the night sky. It all looks so very ordered and tranquil. But there is much chaos in what is seemingly well ordered and peaceful. Nothing is for sure and nothing is as it appears.

What the Heart of the Young Man Said to The Psalmist.....
Tell me not, in mournful numbers,
Life is but an empty dream!
For the soul is dead that slumbers,
And things are not what they seem....

We live in an era where time honored rules and traditions seem to have lost their value; an era where a life that is lived in integrity, honesty, prudence, forgiveness and face to face communication are nothing more than a whisper, a faint memory, fading fast, then lost to an eternity where we not only forget their value, but ignore them and view them as an unnecessary nuisance in today's world. A friend mournfully mentioned to me recently that he felt like there were no rules anymore, a comment I thought interesting in a world governed by so many rules and laws. Indeed, it does seem like it is a "free for all" with no holds barred and every "man" for his own self and interest. Decency is replaced by obnoxious and boorish behavior.

This is the age of incessant email and text messages; viral YouTube videos and ever-expanding social media that one cannot keep up with. Today's youth, starting at very young ages, are buried in phones, chats, Instagram, Play Stations and an ever-increasing panoply of social media platforms. Billions of messages transmitted in seconds, ostensibly entertaining us and keeping us informed, connected and saving time, yet we have so precious little time for that which is Precious. Some of these messages even instruct us on how to most honorably live our lives. Quotes and encouraging messages abound. Everyone is a philosopher. We wade through the day, the week and life, committing to follow precepts and concepts that will lead to so called success, only to soon find ourselves back in the trenches, untracked, in despair and looking for answers to our daily questions about how to best live our lives, searching for that path that will reveal our Personal Identity and Meaning and Purpose. It seems that we have many questions, but the answers are fleeting. We are torn to the right and to the left (not just politically), torn up and down, inside and out. It sometimes feels like we are fighting a daily war with others and within ourselves. We don't know where to turn so we embrace crutches in our lives. Instead of seeking answers inside, we look for answers outside of ourselves. We turn to rationalization, blame, excuses, strife, drugs and other dependencies. We feel out of sync, out of Balance, if you will, between our intrinsic and basic grounded beliefs, and the rules of so-called "success" in today's world. If only we could make a difference; if we could have Purpose and Meaning; if we could have meaningful outcomes and lessons from the challenges in our lives. It seems that it is just not that easy. It is a struggle. It is difficult to find Balance and Power in this frenzied world. It must be earned. It must be practiced.

What I hope to accomplish with the discussions in this book is that these struggles be recognized, perhaps seemingly in vain, to at least be noble. That we have the courage to ask and discuss the difficult inquiries of life. That as hard as it is to learn and apply the lessons, that we will succeed over a period of time by practicing and implementing these lessons. Our success in modifying our visceral thoughts and therefore our behavior is a long term labour. There is no panacea. There is no magic pill. There is however that noble struggle. It is a commitment to live your life working on getting better and doing better and then, being better. Failure and Success; Triumph and Disaster. Yes, those "two imposters" as Kipling so appropriately named them. They are indeed imposters. Success can make you giddy and dizzy with a feeling of intoxication. Success/Triumph is an intoxicant. It feels good. Failure/Disaster can take you to depression and surrender and even make you suicidal. It too is an Imposter. There is no Balance in those diametrically opposed experiences and therefore there is no real Power in them either. Neither Failure or Success, Triumph or Disaster should elevate or denigrate your Mind and Spirit. Whichever one you get, is just that. It's what you got. No regrets, no excuses, no whining, no outlandish celebrations. It's just life. As difficult as it might seem, you must enjoy what you have each day. Success has many fathers...Failure is a lonely orphan. That is the dichotomy we must parse in our path to Balance and Power.

I recall as a young man entering the business world at the age of eighteen meeting face to face with some of these conflicts and having to come to terms with them. I remember my father saying that there was no such thing as an honest businessman. He was in business for himself and yet at that time I viewed him as an honest person who lived with integrity. It was a confusing message. It was as if he was saying that the only person who could be in business and have integrity was him! It was also very confusing to believe those "Blessed are the poor" pronouncements, when it was so difficult to live that way. Why would it be a good thing to be poor? And it was even more confusing when the new theology of economics in religion proposed that "God made us for success". Which one was right, and which one was wrong? It certainly was more appealing to think that God wanted us to be rich than to be poor. But there was that question again. Which is right and which is wrong? I also remembered the Biblical accounts of the difficulty of a rich man going to heaven versus a camel "passing through the eye of a needle". They were confusing and contradictory messages. Yet, I felt an affinity for business and wanted to engage in it. It seemed to be in my blood. In fact, my father and brothers would tease me because I liked dressing up when possible and putting on an old worn out tie. They called me "the businessman". However, I quickly discovered that there were indeed many challenges to being in business and having integrity. Although not impossible, it was a challenge. I was torn between the near euphoria of "closing a deal" and the things that I had to do to be successful. To be fair, there was nothing that I had to do that was dark or dishonest, but there were gray areas passed off as "promotional" that made me uncomfortable. There is an old story about a man who was accused of lying to get a deal done. He responded. "I didn't lie. I stretched the truth for promotional reasons"!! In time I discovered that in business, love and war, the truth is stretched if not outright ignored. While I had the great blessing of experiencing the beginnings of Balance and Power as a very young man, this was my first experience in the real world and it set me upon a path that was and has been a lifelong instruction in doing the right thing. And sometimes the struggle is to know what exactly is right and what is wrong despite what we are trained and conditioned to believe. It should be an easy exercise, but in reality, there are many hazy and blurry lines between what is accepted as right and what is "known" to be wrong. We will discuss Right and Wrong, later. Right today and wrong tomorrow; Wrong today and right tomorrow.

Notwithstanding, for 40 plus years in business I followed the rules, I paid my taxes even on cash income and I never ran afoul of the law or got in trouble.... *until I did.* I illegally routed funds from a loan at my bank, telling them the funds were for project "A," and instead used them for another project, "B," I was indicted, convicted and served two years in a Federal prison. I thought I could make my own rules. The government disagreed. It was an experience that cleared my vision. I thought I was somehow impervious and above the fray. Everyone in prison thought they were above the law. They all knew they were breaking the law, yet they made choices that resulted in prison. The experience was instructive and cathartic for me. The experience fine-tuned my view of Balance and Power, Purity of Intent, Inquiry, Listening, Right, Wrong and so many other elements in this book. My earlier book, "Entheos, God Within", recalls some of my thoughts before and during my time in prison and includes other writings and personal reflections. Going to prison is a very different reality and may differ from your perspective. As I view that time in prison, I would not trade it in exchange for not going to prison. It was an experience that I needed in order to have a complete life experience. Just as spirits cannot complete their journey until they have this human experience, my life would not be complete without having had that experience. That is how profound the days and nights in prison were for me. It would be a rich gift if everyone could have such a revelation in their lives. Therefore, I pose this question. Was my going to prison a Failure or was it a Success? Those two Imposters.

Early in my business career, I had the good fortune to know a most attentive and interesting Mentor who introduced me to some very fine forms of communication. His name was Robert Mares. He taught me some very special and valuable skills which I now understand to be "art forms". He taught me the art of "inquiry" and its sibling, the art of "listening". These two skills are so closely related that they are virtually inseparable if they are to be employed effectively on a 90/10 basis, Inquiry being the 10% and Listening being the 90%. They are like the dual faced Roman god Janus (from whom the month of January derives) who looks both backward to the last year and forward to the coming year.

Both Inquiry and Listening are science and art, and like science and art can be learned and are beautiful to observe, study and experience.

This mentor also taught me how to learn, how to teach, and also how to teach others to teach. The art of teaching is the art of sharing. Learning and teaching require the application of the art of Inquiry and the art of Listening. All these art forms are related and inseparable; synchronous and symbiotic.

I owe him a great amount of gratitude for having shared those art forms with me. As I said, these art forms can also be referred to as sciences. I have always thought that art and science are more related than disparate. Much like boxing is known as the "sweet science", it is, to the studied observer a true art, although it occasionally manifests itself as brutal. A skilled pugilist engages in a magnificent performance; a dance that is a give and take, that when employed effectively produces a remarkable performance. I don't watch boxing for the brutality it sometimes produces, but for this expression of science which very few fighters ever learn and apply, and which most observers never appreciate. The skilled pugilist watches his opponent (listens) and feels him out with feints, moves and jabs (inquiry), to see how the other boxer reacts (more listening). While we may not wish to admit it, we do the same things when courting a new love or when positioning ourselves for a raise or promotion. I prefer the term "art form" or simply "art", because when employed with Purity of Intent, it has a more spiritual relationship and meaning. We should also be cognizant and understand that we are always positioning for something. There is always some underlying motivation for every act even if it is subconscious. Additionally, we justify these acts and thoughts. As Humans, we are the great rationalizers. Everyone, from the Dalai Lama to your banker, is interested in some result; some ultimate goal. The Dalai Lama (Tenzin Gyatso) may be interested in raising your awareness of self with no seeming benefit to himself, while the banker may be trying to keep her portfolio of loans within certain limits to maintain the fiscal integrity of the bank. Both are admirable efforts. But it is your Purity of Intent in what you think, say and do that makes the effort meaningful. For what reasons **other than your own benefit and aggrandizement** are you saying and doing what you say and do? What is your true intent? Sifting through your thoughts, motivations and acts to determine your true intent is an exercise in Reconciliation and Discernment. There can be an underlying and subliminal benefit. That is not to say that the subliminal benefit is dark and not in trust. It is merely a statement of which we must be cognizant to act in Purity of Intent, which provides Balance and Power.

It is natural for us to want to improve our lives in many ways. The goal is to do so with integrity and character. In this way we can establish the basis for gaining Balance and Power and therefore improve not only our own lives but the lives of others whether they are loved ones or total strangers. Later, we will discuss Purity of Intent as it relates to Balance and Power. We will also discuss how the Dalai Lama and Mother Teresa receive(d) more than they give/gave, even when they have been selfless and live in Purity of Intent.

For most of us, our first mentors were our parents, each with their own special messages and teaching. Sometimes these messages were expressed by example and sometimes verbally; sometimes overtly and other times in a subliminal manner. My father introduced me to the wonderful world of words, etymology and semantics; the meaning of words, their origins and specificity as well as philology. My father and mother also taught me ancient Spanish "dichos" or "refranes"; (in English "refrains" or "epigrams"). To a young man they were the *Wisdom of the World* in a few chosen words. I loved those teachings in short phrases. I learned them by heart.

During the school year my brothers and I worked after school, sometimes until early the next morning, then I would serve mass at 6 AM. During the summer we worked in the fields making adobe bricks from 4 AM until it got dark. Somehow in the middle of the day's labor, exhausted as I must have been, I was interested enough to remember these Wisdoms, and later put them to pen and paper. It is apparent to me only now that my parents must have waited patiently for just the right teaching moment, then they shared the appropriate wisdom so as to give it real meaning. I didn't realize what they were doing until much later in life. There is an old saying that *"the older I get, the smarter they get".* Today, I marvel at how many lessons my father and mother taught me that only now I fully realize and appreciate. Many times, the lessons and their meanings don't percolate into the mind and consciousness until much later in life. Don't think that just because your children or friends (and sometimes even your parents) don't seem to "get it" right now, that they won't someday understand. They are listening and watching even if it doesn't seem like it. So, keep honoring those lessons and wisdoms in your daily activities. Someone is watching and someone is learning, and it will be impactful in their lives. This principle applies to everyone with whom you come in contact. Every moment can be a teaching moment. Don't lose the opportunity to change a life and the world. To change one life is to change the world entire.

I am reminded of the character Frank Goode, played by Robert DeNiro in the movie "Everything is Fine". He is a slightly irascible and cantankerous widower who has four adult children, all of whom hide the truth from him for a number of reasons. One of his children, David, on whom he has been very tough and who is a struggling artist and drug addict dies during the course of the movie, but his other surviving children hesitate to inform him. He believes that his son has largely ignored his advice given through talks and conversations when he was a child. He eventually discovers that his son

David has died, and he weeps himself to sleep. He reconciles with his son in his dream and they part, the son to greet his mother, and the father back to this world with his family. Time passes and later he visits the last gallery where his son was selling a painting and finds that it is gone. However, an acquaintance recognizes his last name and finds a painting of David's hidden away. When Frank sees the painting, he realizes that his son was listening after all and it sends a chill and warmth into you all at once. I won't tell you more in case you haven't seen the movie, which I highly recommend. It reminded me that somewhere, somehow, underneath all that noise, distraction and opposition, they are hearing and listening to your message and example. They are absorbing your examples even though it doesn't appear to be the case, even though you don't see the manifestations today. Sometimes their "listenings" manifest themselves much later and when you least expect it. So, don't stop sharing those messages. They are embedded even though we may not yet know how. This concept is true not only for parents and children but for any relationship whether it is a marriage, friendship, business associate or an employer/employee relationship. Obviously, I am not promoting the bothersome nagging type of communication, but rather the meaningful and sometimes subtle messages both in words and in actions. As long as the lessons and messages are based in Purity of Intent, love, acceptance and inclusion, they will survive somewhere in their lives and hearts and souls.

My father also taught me wisdoms in English. This made such an imprint on me that I began to pay close attention to the sometimes-hidden messages contained in them and their practical application to daily living. Later as I moved on and began my own path, I was able to develop the interest and skills in the application of this very special art form. This and my mother's own extraordinary spirit led to the beginnings of the development of Balance and Power in my life.

It is these very special art forms, experiences and thoughts that I am committed to sharing and discussing with you, and all who wish to take this wonderful and powerful journey. It is not a fad, nor is it for those who seek an easy peace. It is a way of life. It is cathartic. It is a glorious struggle. I struggle with these concepts and disciplines every day. It is a life's journey. However, on those occasions when I do succeed, for me, it is a communion with the power of the Eterniverse that can make you Undefeatable. Invictus. It is as if you have an eternal engine within yourself that will never power down. You have this Power within you right now even though you may not know it or recognize it. It is a matter of recognizing that you do have it, discovering it and harvesting it for the betterment of your life's path and the paths of others in your life, and for finally knowing your Meaning and Purpose.

I am reminded of an excerpt from Rudyard Kipling's writings in his poem "IF".

"If you can keep your head when all about you
Are losing theirs and blaming it on you;
If you can trust yourself when all men doubt you,
But make allowance for their doubting too;...
If you can dream and not make dreams your Master,
If you can think and not make thoughts your aim;
If you can meet with Triumph and Disaster,
And treat those two impostors just the same..."
(see the entire poem in the appendix)

I read this poem as a young man and have referred to it often throughout my life. These words are an important message and teaching in the art of achieving Balance and Power. Let us now begin the journey on this life changing "Tao"; the path to Balance and Power in your life as you navigate through this frenzied and troubled world.

Your Book of Life

Every breath is a lifetime

1.

YOUR BOOK OF LIFE

We all live our lives believing that our one individual life we have been given and the life we lead on this earth, in this time and place, in this Eterniverse, is somehow not normal; that it is a crazy life so very different from any other life experience you have witnessed in your friends and even others in your family. Other people's lives seem so normal compared to yours. Your life is a "once in the Eterniverse" life. It is an original and unique life unlike any other. Countless things happen in your own life that no other person will ever know or understand. As you contemplate your life, you understand that your life is so very personal and unique. That makes it special. You sometimes sit back in wonderment at what happens in your life. Nothing could have prepared you for this life. Not your parents, grandparents, your upbringing, religion, culture, traditions or your education. There is no training ground or preparation that could ever inform and teach you about how your life would be. We believe that our life is so unusual and so unlike anything any other human being has experienced or can understand. And it is true! No one seems to really comprehend what we are experiencing. They just don't get it! So, we live our lives with this little secret. We all say, "no one knows how it is with me; my life is crazy; why do I have this crazy life?" Remember the blues song "Nobody knows the trouble I've seen"? Well that's the way it feels, doesn't it? Nobody knows your life and the troubles you've seen. You couldn't make this up!

The truth is that your life is indeed a 'once in the Eterniverse" life. Of the 100 billion people who have been on this Earth, there has never been, there is not now, nor will there ever be a life exactly like your life.

How unbelievably unique is that? Think about that for a second. No other life in the history or future of humanity has been, is now, or will be, exactly like yours. How precious is *that* gift"? Consider that...

The womb of the Eterniverse has given birth to only one of you. **Ever!**

And there will never be another just like you. Only one of you! Not even identical twins who stay together have the same Book of Life. Not even the original Siamese twins, Chang and Eng (Left and Right) had the same life. It really is a miracle. It seems impossible, but it is true. Instead of viewing your life as weird or strange, you should recognize your life as a very special, individual and unequaled experience in this world or any other world. Your uniqueness is, well...unique. There is only one you, which is why you might think your life is a crazy life!! Well, it is a crazy life, but it is the life you got, just like everyone else got their crazy life. It is something to remember when we interact with others. It is important to acknowledge that everyone else also has a crazy life that no one understands. It is a critical evolution in the empathy for others.

Like everything else in life, we can view it as a positive or a negative thing. Light or Darkness? Which lens shall we see this through? We can choose how we see it. If you really think about it, it is hard to see it as anything but glorious and wondrous. There is no other person nor any other life exactly like yours. It is a **singular occurrence** in the Eterniverse as we know it today. Perhaps that is why an encounter with another soul that has Purity of Intent, who seems to "feel" us is so unusual, surprising, and welcome. We are so conditioned to accept the negativity of the intent or ulterior motives of others that when we are blessed with the experience of meeting one of these good souls, we tend to experience doubt about their intentions. We doubt the unexpected sincerity and kindness shown to us. We are suspicious. In fact, if a total stranger came up to you on the street or at the grocery store and just handed you a $100.00 bill, you might take it, but you would probably look around to see what was going to happen (to you) next. People just don't do that. In a very real way, we are conditioned to reject kindness and honesty. We tend to think that there is impending doom in such an unexpected act of sharing and kindness.

How did we become conditioned this way? We ask ourselves, "why would this person do this? He must be interested in something; he must have an ulterior motive, so I had better be careful". But in reality, there is much goodness, kindness and honesty all around us. There are countless acts of goodwill performed each day that we know nothing about because they are not promoted. Positive acts and kindness far outnumber dark acts. Those positive acts are not reported as often as the negative news of the day. Negative news sells.

Positive stories, not so much. So, what should we do with this? It is all about how we choose to live our lives. Do we choose to live in Darkness or in Light?

Getting back to this "vida loca", (crazy life) we all seem to have, I am reminded of the scene at the end of the movie *Tombstone*, when (I paraphrase) Wyatt Earp is asked by Doc Holliday, "what do you want in your life?" Here is the great Wyatt Earp, famous for his exploits, experiencing what seemed like a full and exciting life, handsome and confident; a hero to many and a man most men would want to emulate. A man's man. For a man who has had such a seemingly full and enviable life, Wyatt Earp responds in a shocking manner, "Doc, all I've ever wanted is a normal life." Then Doc Holliday responds without hesitation,

"There is no such thing as a normal life, there's just life."

Sometimes these western movies have the most memorable lines. It seems that they are meaningful as well. I know it's just a movie, but this exchange is profound, and the message is a real lesson.

This deep understanding of the uniquely human experience and condition is a lesson to be learned every day. It helps us to understand that each and every one of the billions of human lives experienced since the beginning of humanity is absolutely unique. Every single person has a unique experience, and every single person wonders, even questions why his or her life's path has unfolded in such a strange and unpredictable manner. Meaning and Purpose is cloistered in there somewhere, and if it is hidden, it means it should be searched for. It is a thing to be cherished, honored and respected. It should make us compassionate of others. It should be cherished that each Book of Life reads differently. How very strange, puzzling and perhaps frustrating, yet how very wonderful. Each one of us has a "Book of Life" written about us and each one of these stories is different and totally unique to each of us. Every word is a unique second and every sentence is a unique minute. Every paragraph is a different hour. Every page is a different day. Each Chapter is a new decade and each book is a unique life. And each one applies solely to you. But it should not be astounding or unexpected when we ponder the countless variables that are present in the Eterniverse that affect how our lives progress and even that our lives exist at all and that we were even born. It is like a miracle. No! It **is** a miracle. Consider the variables that are a part of your existence, of having been conceived and born. All of the variables that could have affected that you were born, and that you exist today are infinite. Everything that happened before you were conceived. Everything, from the trillions of galaxies each containing up to over a trillion stars (suns), our own solar system and the exact placement of Earth in our solar system, the beginning of life on Earth, DNA, and the development of humans who have a conscience and think and are self-aware. Now consider climate, food sources or lack thereof, development of consciousness and self-awareness, geography, countless wars with hundreds of millions of deaths, disease, plagues, weather, migration, accidents, gender, ethnicity, ecosystem and countless other variables that influence our individual birth and Tao; our path. Considering all of the events that occurred or could have occurred precedent to your birth, it is said that the odds of you being born are 1 in 400,000,000,000,000 (one in 400 trillion). I think those odds are far from accurate because there are countless variables in eternity past including the formation and expansion of the Eterniverse, that decrease the chances of you ever having been born, The odds are incalculable. Yet, here you are!!!

For instance, when you look at this from a purely empirical and scientific perspective, you can begin to comprehend how impossible it is that we even exist in this form and in this physical realm at all. For a moment consider how many spermatozoa (sperm cells) are released by a man in one single event, all of whom swim furiously to find the ovum for conception. Can you believe that depending on the individual, from 50 million to 600 million sperm cells are released by a man during one ejaculation? The average male produces an average of 550 **billion** sperm cells in a lifetime. That is one man in one lifetime. Now, multiply that by an eternity before that man and you see why one in 400 trillion is low. A man that produces less than 20 million sperm cells per milliliter is considered sub-fertile, yet each of those has the potential for life.

Once released, the clock starts ticking on the life span of each sperm cell; each on its own mini Book of Life. Then, irrespective of how many sperm cells are released, the ovum has to be ready at that particular time in the woman's cycle to accept the onslaught of hundreds of millions of sperm cells heading toward the egg. The woman's egg is viable for only one day once it leaves the ovary. During all of this crazy activity, each sperm cell has its own life cycle. It is already having its own crazy life. It might zig left instead of zagging right on its travels to the egg. It might get stuck in a bottleneck in a sperm cell traffic jam, and slow down. It might be swimming in circles, or it might be deformed. It might die an early death without ever getting much of a chance to compete for an extended life. Millions upon millions, in fact most of them, don't make it to the ovum, but they do die trying to get there. But that was not you! You kept moving forward. You didn't give up. You didn't die. *Only one out of millions survives!!* After all, it's a struggle to the death for each sperm cell, even early on in the process. When the surviving sperm cells finally reach the ovum, they are probably pretty exhausted and ready to give up the fight. It has been a vicious fight and a long journey after all, with no hotels or rest stops along the way. It is a once in a lifetime rush to life with no breaks. Failure is fatal. Now at the dawn of victory, the survivors that made it safely try desperately to get into the ovum. They struggle, fight, squirm, pierce and do all they can in a desperate effort to survive. Then one of them (only one of the motivated millions) gets through after this really long swim and it drives and drills through the wall employing a chemical solution to penetrate the egg wall. When it gets through, the ovum emits a substance that kills off the remaining suitors. So that survivor is *you* out of millions, and that survival, was really a miracle on its own, and that is just one event where sperm cells were released from one man on one solitary occasion in a life that could have existed and just as easily might never have existed. How many hundreds of billions of sperm cells didn't even have a chance to get to an ovum??!! Yet, you were the one that made it, in some cases, one out of over half a trillion sperm cells in a lifetime from one human male. That is over five times the number of humans that have ever existed on Earth, and that is just from one man. Then you have to go through the whole gestation process followed by birth and a whole unique crazy life thing ahead for one human with all of its unexpected occurrences. In that life, the person might live a long and fruitful life, have one or more offspring or maybe none at all, and maybe die at a young age before having their own offspring thereby denying any future offspring who then have no chance at all to have a crazy life or crazy children. Imagine the billions of events that can occur in that person's life that can affect everything that comes afterward and affect the chances of even having the chance to exist from that potential father.

Stillborn babies	Disease and death
Infertility	Abortions
Accidents	War
Murder	Heart attacks
Earthquakes	Volcanoes
Tsunamis	Etc. etc.

You may experience all of those things and much more, and during all of that a child is born. That is only one "trillion event cycle" in one person's trillion event life that creates an impossible life. Yet it happened. You are here. You exist. I AM!!! Now look back in your family's history for thousands of years and imagine how many of those events in all of those lives before you, had to align at that exact place and time for that whole preceding series of trillions upon trillions of sperm cells leading to conceptions and births to occur for you to even have a chance of being here and alive. Now think about all of the lives and accidental deaths, wars, illnesses and every other element that could affect the matrix that had to be just right for you to be here including the formation of the Eterniverse.

You may or may not believe in the historical context of the Eterniverse as being billions of years old. If you do, then that fifteen billion or more years that the Eterniverse has been bouncing around and pulsating like a living being itself, has produced an infinite (truly infinite) number of potential realities in its own Book of Life that somehow ended up with you being born. Our own Galaxy contains hundreds of billions of stars like our own Sun. Our "local" cluster of galaxy neighbors contains another billion or so galaxies (not stars, but galaxies of stars). Some scientists now believe that there may be over two trillion galaxies in our Eterniverse. I say "our" because again, some scientists believe that there are multiple universes, parallel universes and other universes in other time dimensions. How many explosions of stars, pulsars, red giants, white dwarfs, black holes, collisions, accretions of planets and moons had to take place for the Eterniverse to be what it is today in this exact form? It is unimaginable, virtually incalculable and incomprehensible that even the Earth itself exists today and further, that it exists in a form that allows for life to exist in any form and especially in your form as you exist today.

Ahhh...yes! Life. Your Life. Your unimaginable life....

When you calculate the odds, it is truly a miracle you are here at all. That is why I call it a "once. in the Eterniverse" life. Some people might view that as us being insignificant in the grand scope and plan of the Eterniverse. Instead, I see it as a special gift and that each of us is indeed a unique miracle and *indispensable to the Eterniverse*; If there is a multiverse, there is an Eterniverse. It is an eternity of universes.

You are indispensable to the Eterniverse. You are a requirement for the Eterniverse to exist. The Eterniverse could not exist without you. If it could have existed without you, it would have, but it couldn't exist without you, therefore it doesn't. The Eterniverse had to have you in it in order to be complete. We know that because you are here in it. You are integral and necessary to the existence of the Eterniverse.

So why shouldn't we each have our own Book of Life like no other? We should have a unique Book of Life, and we do.

While some may embrace this uniqueness and singular life experience, many sometimes view it negatively and may honestly confess to exasperating feelings:

"Why is my life like this"?
"This life is crazy"
"This is not what I planned"
"Why am I here?"
"What is my Purpose?"
"This is not what I expected".
"Why is this happening to me"?
"How did things end up this way"?
"Why can't my life be *normal* like everyone else's"?
Really? Normal? What exactly does that mean?

When my mother was pregnant with her second to last child, we were all very excited to have yet another addition and blessing to our already big family. For my mother it was another gift and miracle from God, and she glowed with love, wonder and expectation. When she was about eight months pregnant, she had a horrible nightmare one night. She awoke in a panic and in total fright, clutching her bosom. She screamed in Spanish to my father, "alguien me quito´ algo!" (Someone has taken something from me!). My father tried to console her and asked her to calm down and he asked her to tell him what had happened in her nightmare, but he assured her that it was indeed, only a nightmare. My mother said "the baby Jesus came and took my baby from me. He came into the room and walked beside the bed and took my baby. I tried to stop him, but he took my baby." After she had calmed down and began to rest, she eventually fell asleep again. When she awoke the next day, she felt ill. She visited the doctor and the doctor gave her the news. The baby would be stillborn. She knew it before he told her. Her name is Angelita and she is still to this day our little angel, our Messenger.

My Mother could have blamed herself or complained or asked, "why did this happen to me"? Instead, after some time, she was pregnant again. While she spent some sleepless nights, as did we, wondering if she would lose another child, she gave birth to my youngest sister Felissa, now deceased, and then my brother Joshua, who is also my godson. Both have been blessings to our family, and yes, part of our crazy lives.

The question is, "Do you choose Light or Darkness?" We identify with things, both positive and negative. Seek the Light.

Clothe yourself in the Light. Learn to derive Power from adversity.

The strange thing is that everyone is asking the same questions. This is possible because along with this unique life you have, you are also blessed with a Mind, Conscience, Spirit and cognitive thought and emotions. I can assure you that our most revered American leaders such as Abraham Lincoln, George Washington, Dr. Martin Luther King and John F. Kennedy had these thoughts as did prominent persons throughout history and countless cultures. Yet one would not stop to think or imagine that those people experienced doubt about their place and role in the world. During their times of crisis and challenge, each of them must have felt like this was definitely not the original plan they had imagined for themselves. This was not the way it was supposed to be. Imagine for a moment what each of these people might have asked about their unique path and singular One of a Kind, Book of Life.

"Why is it set unto me to save the Union, or to suffer its demise"?

"How can this be that I am to win this war with ill equipped, starving volunteers"?

"How did this happen that I am to lead a people to the promised land"?

"How could it happen that I must make decisions that could destroy the world"??!!!

Each of these people must have thought it unfair at the time, even though they were committed to their respective causes and probably even had awareness of their place in history and that their Book of Life would be different and unique. But as humans we can't help but feel like we are outside the ordinary course of normal human affairs. To put it bluntly, we kind of feel picked on. Why me?

Mother Teresa, whom everyone "knew" was an unshakable pillar of faith, we now know was doubtful of her own path as reflected in her writings. It seems that she was unsure of her calling. This seems inconceivable. Yet, she expressed her doubts about her path openly and truthfully. One would never imagine that a person of such stature and immense strength would have had any doubts or fears about her position or path; her Purpose and Meaning in life. It is hard for us to imagine that others including our neighbors, fellow employees or bosses experience the same feelings and doubts, many times because they seem like they have it all "together". But viewing from afar can create many distortions. Things are not what they seem. The reality is that we all do have those thoughts. We can see the outward visuals but not the reality of their lives or their thoughts, hopes, desires, fears or their perceptions. The reality is hidden behind a façade which fools us. The interesting thing is that we are all doing the same thing. We try to show a side that hides rather than reveals the underlying truth. So, others look at us and, believe it or not, they think we have a "normal" life; that we have it together.

This is done by design and we are conditioned to do this on many levels including religious, political, patriotic, cultural, business and traditional levels. There is an old saying in Spanish.

"Caras vemos, corazones no sabemos." Paraphrased, it means,
"We see the face, but we don't know the soul (heart)"

We read about those chosen people who have it all. Fame, money, reputation and all of the things most people seem to want. Yet some of those people who have it all commit suicide. Why would they commit suicide? I submit to you that they do so precisely because they do in fact" have it all." It is the "Not having it all" and the "Not knowing what happens next" that gives us Purpose and Meaning in life. Imagine having it all and knowing everything that happens next...There is no Meaning to Life and no Purpose for living.

It is the struggle and the not knowing, that gives us Purpose and Meaning

So, how *did* it come to this? How did we get to this unique life as a part of the miracle that we exist at all?

I recall a very revealing conversation I had with a close friend of mine whom I have mentored for many years. He was caterwauling about how hard things were with his business and how his rentals weren't doing as well as he would like; how he had to replace his old Mercedes, and his house on the hill needed repair and he had a difficult time paying the mortgage, all in the face of trying to keep up his tuition payments for his kids in private school. He then said, "and I can't understand why everyone thinks I'm rich!!!" I responded, "well that's because you *are* rich". He is a very animated guy and he objected to my statement. "If people only knew what I have gone through," he said. I then explained to him how others viewed him. I said, "You have your own business. Ninety nine percent of the population dreams of having their own business and the benefits that come with it, but they fear the risks. (what they don't realize is that it's three times the work of a "normal" job, but with all of the risk). You drive a Mercedes Benz. Even though it is an older model, most people can only dream of owning one. You live on the hill overlooking the city. People don't think about the payments and the cost of upkeep of your house on the hill, they just know that you live on the hill. Your kids attend a private school. Only rich people can do that, right? To anyone who doesn't have what you have, challenges and all, you are rich". I reminded him that he should never forget that, without being ostentatious, he is rich. Of course, I'm referring to monetary wealth here and not the real riches we have which have nothing to do with money, physical possessions, status and the like. He is also blessed with a wonderful wife and children. When he thought about it, and engaged in Perspective, he was able to realize how others see him and how he could be seen as being rich and that in fact he was rich. Yet in his mind he just wanted a normal life. One that in the white picket fence of life, there is only peace and harmony. Hmmm, peace and harmony. Well, think again. He was almost angry that his life was so hectic and had so many unpredictable curves, yet everyone considered that he had the life of a rich man. If they only knew what he went through every day in his Book of Life!! If only it could be that life could be predictably perfect.

How scary would it be to know the future of your life in every detail! How absolutely frightening would it be to know in advance, every chapter and verse in your Book of Life. It is the "not knowing" that gives life value.

Nonetheless, you may ask yourself,
"Why is my life so different?"
"You can't make this stuff up"!!
"I can't believe what happens in my life"!
And I'm sure you've heard this one. "I should write a book about my life. It's been so different"! Well, perhaps you should write a book about your life. The introspection might be interesting.

So here we are, each one of us living this unique life that has only happened once in this Eterniverse. We make thousands of large and small choices in reaction to and as a normal part of this life experience. We don't think about it when it comes to others. Consider for a moment that great or small, each person makes thousands of decisions that can change the world and set it on a new path. We have no idea what is happening right now that will reverberate throughout history. It could be something you did today. A small act, failure to act or decision you made that will change the world. An act of kindness, mercy, forgiveness, appreciation, despair, anger, envy or even apathy. Perhaps you are a mentor to others. You certainly are an example to others whether you know it or not. That makes us all a great part of everyone else's life too, even though we probably don't know them or will ever know them. That makes us all integral, all related. Each one of us to every other one of us. In Lak Ech Ala K'in; "you are my other self". What we remember are the historical choices and the lives of historical persons, but we may never know or understand the butterfly effect we have on the world and its history. Just because you don't know it, doesn't mean it doesn't exist. Remember that Truth exists regardless of our beliefs.

How utterly awesome and incomprehensible that each of us is so unique and one of a kind, that nonetheless, we are all a part of each other and together make one whole Eternal Being and Existence. It is a mystery to be enjoyed.

Abraham Lincoln made decisions about the country, war, life, death, slavery and others that might be unimaginable to us. When elected President, after failing to win previous elections, he must have thought, "I got elected for this? This was not the plan". He probably gave his Gettysburg Address thinking that his words would be long forgotten.

"The world will not long remember", he said.

His Book of Life tells a different story.

George Washington led a struggling quasi organized assemblage of ill-equipped colonies and paid mercenaries to win independence against unreasonable odds. No one should expect this of him, he must have thought. What might he have thought about why he had "this life of mine."? Somehow his decisions worked to gain independence and survival for the new colonies. It could very easily have been different. The formation of the new nation was written in his Book of Life, but he didn't know that when he was living through and blinded by the pages that often spelled seeming doom and defeat.

Dr. Martin Luther King, sensing his destiny in his own Book of Life must have wondered how he could have arrived at that place and time in history. Notwithstanding premonitions of his death, he moved forward toward his final earthly acts, paid his final debt and changed the world. Any minor change in his timing, lodging at the Lorraine Hotel or in his schedule could have changed the outcome. It was written in his Book of Life to happen as it did. How do we know that? Because that's the way it happened.

John F. Kennedy and the Cuban missile crisis were center stage to the potential annihilation of humankind. What was he thinking? "Why is this happening to me?" How could the future of the world rest on his shoulders and depend on his every move? One bad (or good) instantaneous decision could change humanity. How could one human being in the history of mankind be responsible for that? How could that be fair?

Mother Teresa, immersed in poverty and abject deprivation must have questioned why she had been selected for that life's path. Why couldn't she just have had a normal life? Yet in the midst of the doubt and questions, she inspired millions across the planet and thousands to join her order in the hope of alleviating pain and suffering for millions more. As she walked among lepers and sickly people, not even of her faith, she must have thought "is this what I am called to do? Could I, or should I have taken a different path"?

What is your Purpose and Meaning for existing? Why do I exist? Why am I? What am I called to do, if anything, with this life? I don't seem to fit and life is passing by...

Well, what exactly *is* a normal life? Can you answer that question with authority?

Is it the 8 to 5 job, or are you in business for yourself?
Is it a blue-collar job or are you an executive?
Are you a farmer or rancher, or maybe an importer?
What kind of car does a normal person drive? Domestic or imported?
Do you want to live in the suburbs? Maybe the city is better.
Little Johnny broke his arm. Why him, poor thing!!!
Married, single, divorced, engaged, widower?

I could go on and on with what I think comprises a normal life, but it really doesn't matter because it is "just life." It is, just what it is.

Wouldn't it be nice if we could just know what was in store for us? For many, they just want something perfectly predictable. Something they can count on happening. No nasty surprises like those we get almost daily. How comfortable would that be? Perhaps you would like to write your own Book of Life so that you could know every detail of what will or would occur in your life. Maybe you wouldn't write it, but you would want to know how it reads. But would you really decide to know everything that would happen in your life if you could? Would you really want to know what is written in your Book of Life?

What if you knew everything that was going to happen in your life once you reached the age of reason and awareness? What if you already knew what school you would go to, who your friends would be and the fights you would have with them? What if you knew in advance exactly what day you would break your leg and exactly how it would happen? What if you knew who you would marry and how many kids you would have, their gender and health, and what path they would take, good or bad. What if you knew when your parents were going to die and how they would die and where? What if you knew how you would die and the illness that caused it along with the pain you would suffer, or the accident you would be involved in and exactly how it would happen? What if you knew how you would think and view the world later in life? What if, looking from above, you knew everything that was written, every phrase, sentence, chapter and verse in your Book of Life in advance and you couldn't change it anymore? I submit to you that if you did, you wouldn't last long until you craved the surprises and unpredictability of the real Book of Life. You would want "just real life" as it comes with unpredictability as its most savory course. The ancients said that the gods envy us because we will die someday and because we don't know the future; we don't know what will happen next and that "not knowing" was the essence missing from their existence.

We are the sum total of time and circumstance.

It makes us who we are. I remember the original Star Trek series where the always emotional Captain Kirk was pleading his case for our humanity. I paraphrase here. He said," I can't worry about how things might have been. What should I think? That I turned left when I should have turned right? I need my uncertainty. I need my pain. That's what it means to be human".
Why would we want to have a normal life instead of the Book of Life we get? Instead, we should cherish the unknown and look forward to what this day and life brings us. We would want to live it as it comes to us and enjoy all of it, challenges and all and write and read each line as it occurs, savoring its

spontaneity as a fulfilling feast. It is a daily gift. It is a ***precious unknown*** that we have yet to experience. It is what makes life worth living.

It may be the ultimate gift. In many ways it is the "not having it all" and the "not knowing" that gives Meaning and Purpose to our lives

It is important to remember that everyone else is also living their unique Book of Life and that it has its glorious days and its travails as well. Be kind and patient. Be understanding. Plato said,

"Be kind, for everyone you meet is fighting a hard battle."

Understanding this can bring you Balance and Power. Knowing that it is all "just life" can give you Balance because you have a better understanding of your unique, one of a kind life's path and everyone else you know and meet is experiencing their own unique Book of Life. It gives you Power because you can now embrace without fear the events of your Book of Life that are not yet known as part of your path. So, enjoy, appreciate and respect your one and only Eterniversal Book of Life. It is being written just for you and for no other before, now or ever again. You are an Eternal Being that has no equal.

Virtue, and Life After Death

The subliminal reward

2

VIRTUE, AND LIFE AFTER DEATH

For most people of faith, the beliefs of their respective religions consistently provide a very basic concept. Behave according to the teachings of the faith and you will be rewarded with their particular form of salvation, eternal rest, paradise or rebirth. The interesting thing is that because every mind is a Universe, these after life places and experiences are likely to have different expectations for every person. Despite the dogma of a church, as individuals, it is impossible for all adherents to mentally visualize the experience of the next life and existence to be the same thing. But one current runs consistently through these beliefs and teachings. If you do good you will be saved. I don't believe there is any religion that promotes salvation as a reward for bad behavior or damnation as a reward for good behavior. Yet, we have seen many bad actions be rewarded and good actions be punished, at least here in this world.

But we once again come full circle to what exactly defines bad behavior and good behavior. Again, what is right and what is wrong? Virtually all faiths believe that the rules for what constitutes good and evil were handed "down" to humanity by God or their particular version of the Supreme Being or the Creator. If you have had a child, can you faithfully and honestly state that your child knew the difference between right and wrong as an infant? Can you say that your child or any child is aware by nature of the difference between good and evil? Is a newborn child hardwired to possess the knowledge of good and evil? Is it in the DNA? Or is it nurture, culture, social conditioning and traditions that create the knowledge of good and evil?

The Old Testament says that in the Garden of Eden, there was a tree of the *knowledge* of good and evil. This is interesting because it seems to indicate that there is a knowledge, or to put it in other words, an understanding, of the difference between good and evil. So, if Adam and Eve were like children and innocent of the knowledge of good and evil, they could only acquire that knowledge by eating of the fruit. Until that point, they were oblivious to the knowledge of good and evil.
They were innocent like children; like all newborn children.

Here is another question or situation for you to ponder. Imagine that a child is lost at sea and survives to live on an unknown island where there are no people. You can make up your own story as to how that child ended up on the deserted island. The basis of the question is that the child is not exposed to other persons or their thoughts, actions or beliefs. In this story, there is no physical example, no mental conditioning as to what is right or wrong, no church or elders and no indoctrination into a belief system. This child is totally devoid of any relationship as to what might constitute right or wrong or good and evil. Upon reaching the so-called age of maturity and self-awareness, what might this person interpret as being right or wrong? Would this person have a conscience? Would this person have a concept of evil or good? If they didn't have these concepts to live by, what would be the catalyst, if any, that would commence and develop such a thought process where they were conscious of good and evil? Here is an interesting twist...

Perhaps it is the knowledge of good and evil that develops the conscience

Now change the equation and make the story include two lost children and think about how that can change things. Now, once again change the dynamic to make the lost children one male and one female of the same age and perhaps the results are drastically different. How would they develop the concepts of right and wrong and upon what basis would they do so? The male and female element could certainly affect the outcome of what constituted right and wrong and acceptable and unacceptable behavior. But how would that concept develop in isolation?

But the question remains. If infants are not endowed with the knowledge of good and evil, and if such knowledge is learned, what does that say about our human culture today? How do we explain our systems of justice and governance and upon what are they based at any particular time in history or location on the planet? These questions might explain why there are so many interpretations of what is right or wrong in the world, which are influenced by the diversity of cultures, traditions and beliefs; with each society believing they are right. Wars, religions, politics, disputes...

One can also posit that at the moment a human developed a conscience, that was the moment that he or she gained the knowledge of good and evil and the knowledge of what was right and what was wrong. But how was that conscience developed? A law, rule or mandate by society does not necessarily mean that it is congruous with your conscience. History is replete with examples of an individual's conscience transcending laws or other authoritative dictates. If there were no rules and laws, how would you behave? How do you behave when no-one is looking? What is it that governs your behavior?

Many times, people behave in a manner that is totally inconsistent with your beliefs of what constitutes good and evil. In fact, you may also act in a manner that is inconsistent with what others believe is right or wrong, yet you believe you acted properly. You have rationalized and justified your actions, or you would not have acted in the manner that you acted. That is why there are arguments, divorces, business breakups, lawsuits and wars.

The elements that underly this are the following:

Conscience

Perspective

Justification(Rationalization)

As a result of these three elements, each of us believes that we have virtue, character and integrity. We believe that we are acting in character and integrity, even if we are but fooling ourselves about the Truth. And because we believe this, we also believe that we are justified when viewed from our own narrow Perspective. These are times when we manipulate the conscience into justifying our ostensibly virtuous and prudent actions. We have vivid examples in recent history that evidence this phenomenon. As abhorrent as it might sound, even Hitler's conscience dictated his outrageous actions, which from his Perspective, he was justified in doing what he did. That his conscience was deranged and misguided doesn't change the fact that he saw things from a different Perspective and that he ultimately justified and rationalized his unconscionable actions. It is difficult to imagine that he could have done what he did without him believing that he was right in doing it. That is the really frightening part of Conscience, Perspective and Justification (Rationalization).

My time in a federal prison taught me that these thoughts are a reality. I don't believe there was any person who didn't justify their actions that sentenced them to prison. If the sentence was for drugs, the reasoning and justification was that they needed to feed their family; they didn't know they were hauling drugs or huge amounts of money even though they had been paid ten times their normal rate; it shouldn't be illegal if so many people do it; I was just helping out a friend; I am not a drug dealer; I just did it once; they were just servicing a need and someone was going to do it, if not them; they had no reason to stop me; I got set up; they are just trying to get to the kingpin, etc. etc. I even heard one person state that they were merely pursuing the American dream.

You wouldn't believe the stories I heard about those who said they were not obligated to pay taxes and so they didn't pay and ended up in prison. Yet they argued that they should not have been prosecuted. I can understand a legitimate dispute about taxes, but these were people who refused to pay any taxes, then argued it was illegal for the government to collect taxes.

Why do we do this? The answers are tough to accept. One reason we do this is to reconcile guilt. You cannot be guilty of anything because whatever was done was not wrong or evil. It was not wrong because from your Perspective, the act was justified and therefore Rationalized. And like magic, you have a clear conscience. How impossibly powerful is that process? And without giving it a second thought, we do this consistently throughout our lives.

For others, the reason is the need for salvation. We need to be right so that we can attain salvation. We need Life after Death and to get there we will place ourselves on the highest rung of the salvation ladder by our own Justification. We don't want to miss out on salvation, just in case. Clearly, not everything that anyone does in their lives is always the right and good thing, even from their own Perspective and in their own Justification. But we set ourselves above others. We are justified in doing what we do. How do we appear to others?

Oh!... the gift that God would give us, to see ourselves as others see us...
You would be shocked and maybe embarrassed. We behave from a place of love, hate, envy, greed, fear, aggression, suspicion and other human emotions that govern our actions. Sometimes the motivation for our behavior is well intentioned, yet others may see it as evil and unacceptable. Perspective is a powerful thing. We think, "if people could only see things from my Perspective and my life experience, they would understand..." It is interesting what makes people angry based on their Perspective. If you could see all things from another person's Perspective and Justification, theoretically, you would never have discord. Here is a story about Perspective, how it occurs and the effects it has on us:

Once upon a time, five blind men came upon an elephant. "What is this?"

asked the first one, who had run headfirst into its side. "It's an elephant." said the elephant's keeper, who was sitting on a stool, cleaning the elephant's harness.

"Wow, so this is an Elephant! I've always wondered what Elephants are like." said the man, running his hands as far as he could reach up and down the elephant's side. "Why, it's just like a wall, a large, warm wall!"

"What do you mean, a wall?" said the second man, wrapping his arms around the elephant's leg. "This is nothing like a wall. You can't reach around a wall! This is more like a pillar. Yeah, that's it, an elephant is exactly like a pillar!"

"A pillar? Strange kind of pillar!" said the third man, stroking the elephant's trunk. "It's too thin, for one thing, and it's too flexible for another. If you think this is a pillar, I don't want to go to your house! This is more like a snake. See, it's wrapping around my arm. An elephant is just like a snake!"

"Snakes don't have hair!" said the fourth man in disgust, pulling the elephant's tail. "You are closer than the others, but I'm surprised that you missed the hair. This isn't a snake, it's a rope. Elephants are exactly like ropes."

"I don't know what you guys are on!" the fifth man cried, waving the elephant's ear back and forth. "It's as large as a wall, all right, but thin as a leaf, and no more flexible than any piece of cloth this size should be. I don't know what's wrong with all of you, but no one except a complete idiot could mistake an elephant for anything except a sail!"
And as the elephant moved on, they stumbled along down the road, arguing more vehemently as they went, ***each sure that he, and he alone, was right and all the others were wrong.***

We argue about the details of things when we don't have all of the facts.

Getting back to our discussion, if you add the element of free will into the equation of Conscience, Perspective and Justification, you now have a powerful engine that can take your acts anywhere you please, and as you see fit according to your Conscience, Perspective and Justification.. I am not saying that these traits always result in evil. Evil, as we understand it and accept it, is a possible outcome. In fact, Conscience, Perspective and Justification can result in much good in the world. Many people use their free will, Conscience, Perspective and Justification for the good of humankind and the world. But all of this can make you stop and ask,

are there no absolutes in the world?

With everyone having:

> the individual capacity to decide on an act based on free will;
> the freedom to base that decision on what their conscience dictates;
> the ability to view that decision and act from an individual perspective that one believes is correct; and
> justification for that free will decision and act, as the correct and good act,

In that realm and dimension, you have no absolutes in this existence as to what is absolutely right and good and what is absolutely wrong and evil. In effect, it is a frenzied world where there is no Balance. If you stop and think for a moment, it all seems out of control as if there are no rules anymore. It is such a frenetic life that one can wonder what really matters in this life and in this existence? How can you really depend on anything being consistent anymore? What would become of values and integrity?

I submit to you that it must start within. That the God entity and Conscience that resides inside of you will guide you to doing the right things and to doing those things with Purity of Intent.

Much of what we decide to do is based on temporal satisfaction and on having things. Wanting more material possessions is what drives this frenzy. It is unending.

Apocryphally, John Rockefeller was asked once, "Mr. Rockefeller, you have much property, skyscrapers in New York, banks, businesses...you are the richest man in the world! How much is enough?" He responded, ***"just a little bit more."***

We have discussed this human phenomenon of "having things," or in the alternative, how things "have us." We progress through life always wanting more, and finally learn that on the last day, at the final hour and in the ultimate seconds of our earthly existence, that everything physical is meaningless. How much is one more breath worth? We all have nothing physical left at that moment; not even one more breath. Not our bodies, nor our possessions. It is truly the great equalizer. It is a clean slate; a Tabula Rasa.

Recently, I attended a funeral service for the father of a dear friend. He is Native American, and the service was held (celebrated) in a relatively humble, non-descript "All Nations" church. The service was quiet and full of spirit and humanness. When the invited pastor spoke, he quoted from the Christian scriptures then prayed in Dine, the language of the Navajo Tribe. It was special to be there. However, he said something very meaningful after that. He said, "At the end of our time here on earth, we take nothing with us, no matter how much money, property or possessions we have, you never see a U-Haul attached to the hearse, full of the deceased' possessions, on his way to the cemetery." It was such a vivid illustration that I will never forget it. But it's true. Because we live in the physical realm, we cannot easily escape the clutches of the allure of "more."

My father used to say, "I can't imagine what heaven might be like, because I feel like I'm in heaven right here and now." He was a man who didn't always have an easy life, but somehow transcended it to feel that way.

So, we go through this life searching for what really matters. Why do you want to live a life that has meaning? What exactly is that meaning and purpose? What does it matter that there is meaning and purpose? What is supposed to happen because we find meaning, and live our lives fulfilling that purpose?

Why should we care and why should it matter about how we behave, what we choose in free will and how we justify our life's acts? It is because we want to have Life after Death. It is the argument for another existence. Even though we are bound by the physical world, most people can have another worldly quality that traverses the chasm between here and there. It is a subconscious manner of living, but we have it. You have it. You have virtuous traits such as:

Honor	Courage
Integrity	Faithfulness
Honesty	Forgiveness
Duty	Bravery
Sacrifice	Justice
Charity	Empathy

These attributes have been manifested in your life at one time or another, even though they may have been unconscious acts or thoughts. They are a part of us being **sentient and sapient** beings and part of the universal existence and plan. I like to say that they are "soft wired" into us, meaning that these attributes are part of us, but not integral to our purely physical existence. Again, it is the difference between the Brain and the Mind. It is a yearning to continue to live in a better place after death. You can observe this phenomenon express itself upon the death of virtually anyone as they express their belief in a place after death that is better than this one.

One day I went to visit my Mother, Luciana. I told her I had some fantastic news for her. In great anticipation she asked me what I had to tell her that was so exciting. I then told her, "Mama, I found out there is no hell!" Puzzled and astonished, she admonished me and said that it couldn't be true. "We are Catholics/Christians and we believe that such a place exists," she said. I insisted. "Really, Mama, I found out there is no hell!". Starting to listen to me, she asked me where and how I could have found this out. I told her, "I saw it in the Sunday paper." "In the Sunday paper?", she asked. "Yes, I saw it in the Sunday paper." "Que dices", she asked. ("What are you saying?"). I then told her I saw the evidence in the obituaries. Now she was totally confused, but she listened, nonetheless. I continued, "I saw in the obituaries that Joe Smith went to eternal rest, and Mary Chavez is in heaven, and Sophie Pierrot was taken by the angels to paradise, and Walter Clarke is in the kingdom of God. There were 25 obituaries and not a single one said, 'that SOB went straight to hell!'. Every single one of them went to heaven!" She said, "well, I never thought about it that way, but it's true; they all go to heaven; none of them goes to hell."
By the way, that is a true story.

I wondered why we think and behave in that manner. I believe that it manifests a deep-rooted hope that we can't imagine that someone we loved, even if they were an incredibly difficult and intolerable person in life, would go to eternal damnation, no matter how terrible they might have behaved while alive. At their death, when we come to terms with their (and our) eternity and the possibilities of what they might face in life after death, we have a hard time accepting that their soul could be condemned for all eternity. It is simply too much to accept. Ultimately, we believe that we are all made for salvation and some form of rewarding existence after death.

It is this acceptance of human frailty and the recognition of human virtues that give us the connection to existence after physical death. It gives us hope. That there is forgiveness and redemption. These virtues are the metaphysical bridge that operate on a different level, that we sometimes don't comprehend or accept. They are an argument, a reason, to understand that there is another reality that you don't want to miss out on. What matters? What does it matter that you "lay down your life for your fellow man," if there is no reward in the next life? Why sacrifice your life for another, if sacrificing everything you have and everything you are ever going to have, has no reward? Would you still do such a thing if you "knew" there was no life after death? Would you act in a virtuous manner if you knew there was no life after death?

We have all read, seen or heard the now familiar accounts of people running into the burning building to save a child, or someone diving into a river to rescue a drowning person, and giving up their lives in so doing. Have you ever stopped to think, (I'm sure you have), how you would act or react in such a situation? I think we all have.

Some would say, "I would do the same!" Others would say " I just don't think I could do it."

The reality is that we don't know what one will do in those situations regardless that there may be a reward in a life after death. What would that person be thinking? What would be going through their mind in that instant when one decides to act at their own peril? What is the motivation, if any?

Is it fear or is it courage, that moves or makes us still?
(from Enthéos, God Within)

In the movie Hart's War, Colonel William A. McNamara who is prisoner of war and is the leader of the other prisoners, makes a calculated decision over a period of time that he knows will take his life, even though his fellow soldiers are unaware of it. He consciously gives his life so that his soldiers will be spared. He trades his life for theirs. But why would someone do that unless there is a promise of reward or some other justification? Otherwise, why do anything at all if it doesn't matter; if there is no positive or negative reward or punishment?

Perhaps, we have the ability to ***do good without the hope of reward***. That is Purity of Intent. It is Godliness. Yet, while we may not fully comprehend it or perhaps not fully believe it (or believe in it), the inner commitment and motivation to sacrifice yourself, whether in an instant or as a conscious decision, argues for the hope and expectation, whether outright or subliminal, of another life or reward.

In what may seem anathema, some of the best people I know who act in integrity, sacrifice, sharing, honesty, forgiveness, empathy and love, do not believe in a God entity, salvation of a soul or an afterlife. They act in this manner with no expectation of a reward in a life after death or any other reward, because they don't espouse that belief. That too, is Purity of Intent. Some argue that a non-believer will behave in greed, anger, revenge, envy, bitterness, fear and other negative characteristics, because there is no fear of consequences or of retribution.

I have not known that to be true by any measure.

By understanding the impact and the role that virtues play in our daily lives, we can access their Power in our lives, in each decision we make and even in our every thought. This gives you Balance by understanding that while we are physical beings, we can act and think in an enlightened manner to oppose the frenzy in the world, regardless of whether we might or might not receive a reward.

Purity of Intent

Cleanse your mind and soul with pure intentions

3.

PURITY OF INTENT

What is your intent when going through your daily routine? Is it intended to produce the maximum gain only for you? Does it ignore that there are others that can lose or benefit from your actions? What exactly are your intentions today?

Most of us have been raised in some manner of a religious or spiritual belief system. I have often thought about the very first self-awareness, religious or spiritual belief a human experienced. The basic platform and original intent of most of these belief systems is fairness, equity and honesty with the ultimate goal of some form of salvation, rebirth, enlightenment or spiritual and even physical transformation, whether it be re-incarnation or the resurrection of the body. Of course, there are some who do not believe in any form of existence after physical death and give no credence to a Mind and Spirit apart from the physical body.

Some manner of Reconciliation is espoused in most belief systems. Reconciliation comes in different forms and it appears that Reconciliation is a generally positive construct. I can't think of a single mainstream spiritual belief system that when applied in its true and originally pure intent, espouses violence and acrimony as its basis, and condemnation as its goal. Sadly however, good intentions seem to vanish as a religion develops a following, grows its membership, and requires infrastructure to manage its growth. Many believe that their religion was founded by God, yet all religions undeniably have a human fingerprint. Through the belief that God founded the faith, humans also developed the rules, promises of salvation and threats of damnation, excommunication, tithing and all manner of rules and dogma. And while they may be very different in their earthly message, they all promise a "heavenly" reward or some other form of enlightenment. What is interesting is that the promise of eternal life and the threat of eternal damnation play such a pivotal role in so many religions. This dualism, which dates to Zoroastrianism, an ancient Persian faith, is now part of almost all religions. Heaven and Hell; God and Satan; Good and Evil; Demons and Angels; Light and Darkness; Salvation and Damnation. The promise of eternal life or the punishment of eternal hell. Think of these promises and threats as methods by which a person can be conditioned to believe in a precept or dogma. Later we will talk more about heaven and hell and how sometimes it all just doesn't make sense. It is interesting to note that the Greek word "Daemon" means both "Messenger" and "Angelos/Angel." It does not mean Demon, as in Satan. Also note that the word "Satan", derived from the Greek "Satanas", means "Adversary." In ancient writings, "God" and Satanas, who was God's companion, tested His subjects to see if they would violate the law of God. Thus, Satanas came to be known as the Tempter in Chief and later, Lucifer and dozens of other names for the "Devil". Because dualism required opposites, Satanas and God became opposites instead of partners such that Satanas was now evil personified as the "Devil"! instead of God's companion. The human construct is amazing in that it creates heaven, hell, God, Devil, light and darkness, good and evil and all of the rules and laws in this world, all in an effort to make you behave in a certain manner. The intent seems to be justified; however, the method is questionable. Seeking the Truth often collides with Faith. That is why we have so many different faiths, religions, churches and wars.

However, there have been many great human beings that have espoused and taught a pure and fulfilling approach to life and our relationships. I believe that most people are intending in good faith to honor these principles and the acts that manifest these ideals. As we all know, it is no easy task. What seems to complicate things here on Earth is that these many religions and beliefs seem to have so many rules and restrictions that it is hard to keep track of them all. If it's not one rule we are breaking, it's another. I have often said that all religions are a buffet in a cafeteria of beliefs. Because we are conditioned, we won't admit it readily, but we pick and choose what fits and benefits us and don't serve ourselves the stuff we don't like; the things that are hard to do. Worse than that, sadly, we forget the true intent of the original teachings. In most cases, what started out simple and pure, transforms into a financial and political structure and empire. That which begins as a pure journey in faith many times ends up in budgets, elections, politics, rules and excommunications. This happens because although a new church may commence its mission with a pure and simple message, if the message is appealing to large numbers of people, it soon requires organization, budgets, leadership, rules and all of the systems attendant to governance, politics and economics. It is, after all, humans who are appointed to do these things here on Earth. Eventually churches even split into subsets due to canon law, inclusion or exclusion of biblical books, discord in governance, interpretation of dogma, financial issues or even scandals. You have Lutheran, Orthodox, Reformed, Eastern Rite, Roman, Coptic, American, Sunni, Ismaili, Shiite and hundreds of other branches of an original faith.

After the Protestant Reformation was sparked on October 31, 1517 by Martin Luther's posting of the 95 theses at the Castle Church in Wittenberg Germany, the resulting unintended consequence would be the creation of thousands of Protestant churches. There is always some different way to interpret the so-called original and governing writings of the faith, whatever that faith may be. What is the need and basis for 20 interpretations of the Bible, just in English? Why was there a need for a new definition of a word or phrase, and who decided that a new definition was required? Was it incorrect and needed to be corrected? What constituted authority to do so and by whom was such authority granted? Some faiths can't even agree on what is included in the basic writings that govern their faith and church. The Apocrypha in the Catholic Church is a good example. It's good enough for the Catholic Church, but not good enough for Protestants. So, we kind of pick and choose what we read and like and what it means to us, cafeteria menu style. Maybe that's not all bad, it's just an observation. Things do mean different things to different people. That's being human.

After all, every Mind is a Universe unto itself

I was having a discussion with a friend about certain writings of different faiths including Catholicism. The topic turned to a writing in the Book of Wisdom which is a favorite of mine. She said she had never heard of the Book of Wisdom. I said, "I'll go get my Catholic Bible and read it to you." She asked, "what do you mean, the Catholic Bible?" I said, "Well my bible is a New American Bible version of the Catholic Bible. I could see the blank look on her face and that she was really having a difficult time getting her arms around what I had just said. It was as if I was speaking a language she didn't understand. She wanted to know what I meant by a "version" of the Bible. She was in disbelief.

When I explained to her that there are many versions of the Bible in many different languages and that they all have differences in their writings and even differences in their interpretations and meanings, she was not only in disbelief but also was very dejected. She was very saddened by this revelation. She always thought that "the Bible is just the Bible" and that God wrote it. That was the one thing she knew she could count on as factual and true. Not willing to yield to disbelief, I showed her that the Book of Wisdom was not in her King James version of the Bible. She was incredulous. I didn't even get into the fact that succeeding interpretations of the original writings have been in dispute practically since they were written and that the New Testament writings weren't even reduced to writing by the apostles to whom they are attributed. The Gnostic writings, the Apocrypha and Septuagint are examples of those different interpretations and discrepancies.

It can get very confusing and exasperating with all of the variations on a theme. Doesn't it seem like a belief or principle should be universal? Shouldn't it mean the same thing to all of us, especially since these writings are ostensibly inspired and universal? Everyone thinks that they have the "answer" or the "one true faith". Some people even "know it". I have visited many people who have stated in a very matter of fact way that their religion was the only true faith. To them, there is no allowance for anything but their own beliefs and faith. In fact, they are on a "salvation list" of some definite number who will be saved upon the coming of the Savior. While I respect people's beliefs and while it is commendable that one can have a strong belief system, it also breeds contempt for any faith or belief that doesn't agree with theirs. There is no tolerance for differences. We build mental and spiritual walls and imprison ourselves unnecessarily. And we wonder why so many people have been killed over religious beliefs. It's the opposite of what should be happening. However, there is a lot of good to be said about total commitment too. There is an old saying, "You have to stand for something, or you'll fall for anything". But shouldn't there be Balance in this equation as well? It all seems so simple, but it isn't. Faith and Fact raise their heads in a mutual dispute over what governs. Faith and Fact are anathema. If you have one, you don't need the other. If I have the Facts, I don't need Faith. If I have Faith, I don't need Facts. It is a dichotomy that creates much discord.

At the same time, I see people who are saintly and who adhere so fervently to an established religious faith that I can't help but admire the manner in which they live their lives and follow their chosen religious tradition for the betterment of their own lives and the lives of others. They really make their path a daily way of life and their actions speak to their beliefs instead of their words speaking to their actions. They are selfless. They have strength, tolerance and acceptance. They are intrinsically good human beings. My mother, Luciana was such a person. (By the way, the name Luciana, Lucy, Lucille, Lucia and all of those related names come from the Latin "luce", or "light." In fact, in the Christian tradition, the name of one of God's great angels was Lucifer, which is a derivative of this word. He was the "Angel of Light"). I'm sure you can think of such saintly and pure people in your life. It almost seems that they don't have to try to be good and do good. They just seem to be good people and behave that way all of the time. It comes naturally to them. They are pleasant, smiling, forgiving, sharing, loving and every other good trait you can define. We almost envy their ability to live their chosen faith as part of their daily lives. (It's enough to make a person angry!) As for the rest of us, we try, and we succeed, and we also fail quite often, some more than others. It is all a lesson in living our lives and truly seeking Purity of Intent. We want to live our lives in integrity. We even succeed many times. We do have success, but we also fail, sometimes even when we think we are succeeding

I submit to you that the successes are those inspiring moments when we act with Purity of Intent. When you behave in that manner, you can also have Enlightenment because in your conscience…

"you did the right thing for the right reasons"

You feel glorious and strong. You feel the Balance and Power within you, although it is sometimes a fleeting feeling and emotion. Unfortunately for most of us, it seems to be a daily struggle. Not just a daily struggle, but a struggle all day. Even having a negative thought about someone, saying something negative or being a little envious makes us feel like we have to start all over again. We feel like we've failed, but we must keep trying; trying to get to that transcendent level if even for a moment and even if only once in a while. You only fail if you stop trying. Fight one more round and you can't lose!

The failures, which I prefer to call "learning", gnaw at us. The whole concept of failure should be re-worked. I think it's overrated. Don't misunderstand, I'm not one of those new age "nobody fails" kind of people where everybody gets a prize, and nobody comes in second. Yes, in the real world we have success and failure. But a failure is a foundation if a lesson has been learned. If you view it and treat it that way, and if you act upon the lesson, there can be success in failure. Remember those two Imposters? We have all heard the all too inspiring accounts of so many who "failed", then won against all odds. One of our greatest Presidents, Abraham Lincoln, comes to mind. He failed in some ways most of his life. In a very real way, those failures established the foundation for the success that was to follow in his Presidency, the preservation of the Union and the Emancipation of Slaves. His so-called failures actually prepared him for the immensely difficult task of preserving the Union. Someone who had always succeeded might not have had the mettle, conditioning and endurance required of such a task. If we fail at something, it is really discovering successfully what doesn't work. Its sounds a little packaged, but it really is true if you choose to see the Light and live in the Light instead of the darkness. It's our choice.

Most of the time we know through our innate goodness and our knowledge of what is right and what is wrong what we should have done or said in certain circumstances, but instead we may have Surrendered. It is, what we believe in a world of "free choice", a conscious decision to travel one path over another. You turned left instead of turning right. How did that affect not only your life but the history of the Eterniverse? The paths seem blurry sometimes, and we may choose the proverbial path of least resistance or the path that provides instant gratification. We have an idea and then we choose a path. Who is responsible? What is responsible? It has been said that

"an idea is not responsible for the person who believes in it".

There is more discussion later about our concepts of right and wrong and also about the whole idea of Causation, free choice and free will.

Surrender. Is it a conscious choice or does it just happen without our involvement? For those who believe in Determinism, it can be said that they believe that it is almost as if the act of Surrendering, making the wrong choice or anything that happens, is independent of us because it was pre-determined; that we aren't involved in the process. It seems, or perhaps we want it to be that Surrender is independent of our conscious thinking and decision-making process. It seems that you and the act are not responsible for one another. It's natural for this seeming disassociation to exist. We reject our Surrender act as if some other being or force had been responsible. This is one of the philosophical arguments with the Mind and Body problem. In other words, we don't want to accept responsibility when we Surrender to an act that is not consistent with Purity of Intent. Yet we may know in our deepest and most profound being and conscience that we didn't act with integrity. This must be Reconciled. But it is difficult because we humans are the greatest justifiers on the planet. We can make a reason or excuse for anything we have done. We can justify anything. It is about our Perspective; the way we view things solely from our point of view. It is a powerful thing. I witnessed the power of Perspective while in prison. Most prisoners had a firm belief that they had been treated unfairly, that what they did was not a punishable offense and in fact they shouldn't be in prison, while the correction officers had no compunction to show compassion or understanding.

The Creator has given us tools to discern Perspective. One of them is your dreams. Your dreams will reveal these subliminal thoughts to you if you lay down your mental armaments and defenses and allow them to speak to you truthfully and without resistance from your inner mind. Dreams rarely talk to you directly. Mostly they communicate in parables and strange symbolism. They come in the strangest forms and messages and seem so very convoluted. We disregard all too readily and our peril these potent messages. But it takes courage to accept the messages your dreams are trying to convey to you. It is a natural form of Reconciliation if you allow your dreams to talk to you. Most people dismiss dreams as some sort of nebulous occurrences that have no real meaning in our lives. I submit to you that your dreams can be the single most important portal to peace, acceptance and reconciliation in this physical existence, if you learn and allow the messages contained in them to speak to you without fear of knowing the truth and the revelation of things you will not acknowledge to yourself in your waking hours. Sometimes your dreams tell you what you won't admit and what you don't want to know about yourself or what you are thinking subliminally. This is an exercise that you should try. At first, you will be lost wondering "what the heck did that mean? It couldn't really have meant anything, could it? It doesn't relate to anything in my life." But think about the symbolism in the dream, not the seemingly obvious message. Try to connect the symbolism to something you fear or love or are worried about. It takes time to read those messages, but I assure you that they are there if you allow yourself to be honest. Why do we fear the truth? We shouldn't fear truth, we should embrace it. It does after all exist on its own and independent of what we believe, whether we accept it or deny it. The Truth does not need us to approve of it or acknowledge it in order for it to exist. I talk about dreams because they are gifts to us, and they are free. Dreams can be your own personal therapist if you try and learn from them. Imagine that!!! You have your own personal therapist inside you! Self-analysis, reconciliation and understanding Perspective are possible every day and we should use the gifts we get to achieve Peace and Balance and Power.

The Hopi Indians of New Mexico have a word that means Life out of Balance It is "Koyanisqattsi." I am always amazed, but I shouldn't be, about the wisdom that the ancients understood at the most basic yet enlightened level. I assure you that your dreams can take you to a new level of understanding, and of Balance and Power if you allow yourself to understand and enjoy the messages hidden in them. Free your mind. Free your body, Free your Spirit. Free yourself from the shackles of dissonance and discord. Make Peace with yourself and make Peace with the Universe.

Getting back to doing the right thing. What about those times when we do good? It is a much clearer picture. It is easy to embrace the successes.

"Success has many fathers; Failure is a lonely orphan"

We know when we acted with Purity of Intent. It is euphoric. No one has to tell us that we did the right thing. We recognize it when it happens. Purity of Intent is acting in a manner that proclaims that regardless of the obstacles, temptations and challenges,

"this is the right thing to do." Do the right thing.

If there were no religions, faiths, synagogues, temples, churches, commandments and rules, you could still act with integrity and with Purity of Intent. You would still know the right thing to do. Is there a difference between the ethics training doled out by government and corporations and the ethics that you already know? If there was no one watching you and keeping a scorecard of your sins, you could still act with honesty, character and integrity. If you didn't believe in the condemnation of hell because of sinful offenses and breaking the rules of your religion, you could still be faithful to goodness, generosity, forgiveness and kindness. The fact that we do have religions, spiritual teachings and faith traditions should only enhance these acts, but it doesn't always work that way. Being pure in your intent is to do no harm as stated in the Hippocratic Oath. If you were an empath, you would feel the feelings and thoughts of another person. You would not likely injure that person physically, financially, emotionally or spiritually, because it would be as if you harmed yourself. Some religions state that

"to harm one person is to harm the world entire"

You have had these feelings. When you see a homeless person, a part of you has no place to go. When you know someone is in prison, a part of you is captive. When a loved one loses a parent, a part of you departs with them. It is these enlightenments that make us one with the Spirit and with all things in this time and place and in all other unknown times and places and dimensions. Remember, "Omnia ab Uno," "Everything from One."

We should embrace the Lessons as well. I refer to failures as Lessons because if we are to sincerely pursue Purity of Intent, we will cultivate an improved behavior from the failures. It has been said that
"failure is nothing more than learning what doesn't work"

Learning what we shouldn't do again or perhaps how to do it better next time. I have counseled people that

"one should neither invent feelings nor deny them"

Your feelings are simply what they are. Whether it is loving someone and not being able to explain the reasons why or feeling guilt for something we have said or done. Many times, we don't want to admit how we feel because we feel like it exposes us to further hurt or risk. We look for excuses as to why we don't really feel something, like hurting because of a breakup, or conversely, why we feel something that we really don't feel, like trying to convince yourself that you love someone that you really don't love. What does it benefit us or others when we invent a false feeling or emotion or deny a real feeling because we are fearful that admitting it would make us weak, vulnerable or guilty? It is far better to acknowledge the feeling or emotion because it is real and truthful. Doing so allows you to Reconcile the feeling and therefore understand it in Truth and at its face value. It is important to also share the truth and honesty with others. After all,

"the Truth is still the Truth whether we acknowledge it or not"

For instance, if you have been hurt in a relationship, you can easily clutch into denial of the feelings of hurt and love you are still feeling. You might say, "I'm glad we parted ways. I don't miss her". "I'm not really hurting over her", or some other form of denial. This can only fester if you don't acknowledge these feelings. It would be healthier for your spirit, heart and soul to acknowledge the pain, anger, hurt and even humiliation, if that is what you are feeling. Acknowledging that feeling or emotion is what is required for the start of the healing process. It is a truthful and unvarnished Reconciliation with yourself that only you can accomplish. In this manner you neither deny nor invent feelings that have no basis in reality. This is something you can do every day. This form of self-reconciliation is a powerful discipline where you can derive Power from discord and pain and make yourself more Powerful, instead of the situation drawing away your Power and making you Surrender.

Seek Power from adversity instead of surrendering your Power to it.

Take the Power from the problem.
Take the Power away from adversity and make it your own.

When it involves acknowledgment of a "failure" in your quest for Purity of Intent, without beating yourself up, simply acknowledging that "I know I can do better", is the new beginning we seek. "I can change my behavior by changing my thinking". How can this give you Balance and Power? You can do this by taking possession, responsibility and ownership of your thinking and your actions. No one else is responsible. Let's stop this insanity of blaming everything on everyone else. This culture of victimhood is devastating our society. Stand up and take responsibility. When the Hebrews were wandering in the desert after their Exodus from Egypt, they celebrated at a ceremony at Gilgal, which to them, meant

"the place where we took possession of our shame"

It was a cleansing and cathartic experience for them that allowed them to move forward on their collective path as a people and culture. It is a lesson that teaches us to live with a clear Mind and Conscience and no baggage. We can pretend, blame and point fingers, but in the end only you are responsible. As human beings, we can rationalize wrong into right and right into wrong. We are very good at it. We are very clever at picking what works for us in our lives and what doesn't. It is part of the cafeteria buffet religion I spoke of earlier. We find all manner of reasons, justifications and excuses for our behavior. However, only I can ultimately change my thinking and behavior and only You can change yours. With no offense to counselors, therapists and other similar professionals, we will not change our behavior until we are ready to do so, although I do believe that a good counselor can open the mind to accept the possibility of modified behavior. When we take ownership of and responsibility for our actions, it creates a feeling that is powerful and overwhelming. It is also very peaceful, and Liberating. Somehow, I was able to take responsibility for my actions and accept the sentence I received. Stand and take responsibility and ownership for yourself and your actions. This gives you Liberation, and Balance and Power!

FORGIVENESS

I have been told by several people that they are aware of two people who reported me to the Federal government authorities. This may or may not be true. Nonetheless it was an opportunity to practice the concepts of which I write in this book; to understand their Perspective and Forgiveness. Employing those two things supported me in my difficult journey.

Forgiveness may be one of the most difficult behaviors to adopt. By this, I mean true Forgiveness. We hear people say, "I forgive you, but God will get you". It is as if to say that you are leaving it up to God to make this person suffer and pay the price, however, you are washing your hands and soul of the dirty business of Forgiveness, just as Pontius Pilate did. What kind of superficial and insincere act is this? It is so shallow as to be laughable. It is not Forgiveness at all. Yeah, I'll just sit back and wait until God punishes you and when He does, it will make me happy. God will take care of it (for me). You'll live with the Sword of Damocles hanging over your head!! There is no Purity of Intent in such a fake forgiveness. I submit to you that it is no forgiveness at all!! This is a Surrender too. Think for a minute about why we do these things. What will usually emerge is an acknowledgement of a powerful emotion. Fear, anger, guilt, envy, greed, love or deceit. Once the specific emotion is acknowledged, a deeper, further understanding of your reaction is in order. It is time to Reconcile this issue. Ask yourself truthfully why you are feeling this emotion. Being truthful even though it is painful, is the only way to arrive at Reconciliation. Meet the messenger face to face without fear of the Truth. Why would we not want to know the Truth? It exists regardless of what you might think is Truth. Consider whether you can manage or control this emotion the next time the opportunity arises, such that you can alter the response or behavior. You will be better prepared for it. You might succeed fully or perhaps just a little at a time. It takes practice and patience and yes perhaps many more so-called failures and lessons. If you sincerely pursue Purity of Intent, your evolution is inevitable. You will become more powerful. You will become passionate about increasing your Balance and Power by a truthful and genuine pursuit of Purity of Intent, especially when interacting with people and also when Reconciling with yourself on a daily basis. "Feeling" another person's emotions is possible with this approach, understanding that they may be fragile. The Mayan civilization had a phrase that captured this level of understanding. Their utterance was "In Lak Ech." (Ala K'in)

YOU ARE MY OTHER SELF

It is also interpreted as

"You are the other me" and

"I am another yourself"

As Luis J. Rodriguez, the author says,

"We are all related. All life, all beings, all things, linked and unified and important"

Again, "Omnia ab Uno". Can you believe this? We consider ourselves so evolved today. In reality we are only now re-learning the beginnings of how to live and think in a transcendent manner. We are fortunate to have remaining glimpses and wisdoms of the past that enlighten us in this way. To have such a concept of unity and the merging of souls while here on Earth seems a new age concept when in fact, it is ages old. I wonder how many other ideologies and ancient wisdoms were destroyed by fear and ignorance that we do not know or have the benefit of and have yet to re-discover.

Acceptance, Understanding and Acknowledgment of this reality result in acts and thoughts that are Pure in their Intent and ultimately in Reconciliation with ourselves without the need for outside input. You are your own therapist. You have God within. You have the Power to heal yourself. We have the answers within us if we will but listen to the Spirit, Entheos, in each of us; the God Within. It is there for you to learn, access and use, but you must have a Listening for it.

Transcendent acts

Purity of Intent

Balance and Power

The life of Lao Tzu was the manifestation of human Purity of Intent. While teaching his "Way of Life", the "Tao" or the "Path", Lao Tzu incessantly endeavored to reduce and eliminate his personal stature and importance as it related to the message and teachings he was trying to convey. For him, the message was more important than self-aggrandizement. It was more important for the teachings and lessons to survive than it was for the memory of Lao Tzu to survive. His intent was pure. That certainly is a different and novel approach. It is the opposite of what we have come to expect from today's preachers. Today's religion features personas of rock star stature, Super Bowl venues, multi-million-dollar homes and jets, all based on the new age dogma of the theology of success, prosperity and economics. Distorting a pure message of love, forgiveness, humility and other pure acts into something that would be unrecognizable to the original Teachers. That was not the case with Lao Tzu. He did not succumb to the inebriation of his high position. I highly recommend that you read his writings. The way of Life... The Dao te Chung or the Tao de Chung.

Speaking of kindness, goodness and pure acts, we have all known people who seemed to be pure and good and kind without trying to be those things. It seems they are rare in our troubled world. My father-in law, Roberto Sanchez was such a person. He was the kind of person that had no malice in his heart. Everything was always just fine. I remember when my father passed away, we had a gathering at my house after the funeral to celebrate his life, as is the traditional custom in the Hispanic and Catholic tradition, and other cultures as well. During a certain time when we had occasion to be alone he put his hand on my shoulder and looked into my eyes with his own serene gaze and said, "don't worry Hito, (son), you still have one daddy left". He said it with such simple sincerity and strength that it was as if it was coming from an angel. That simple and profound kindness has remained with me as a very special event in my life. His was a special and profound touch. He was Balanced and Powerful. May his soul rest in peace. I miss him. It was interesting and inspiring to witness such a person who simply lived his life in peace and purity. It was equally interesting to see that he didn't have to try. It just was who he was. God blesses us in having such people in our world. As for me, as it is for most of us, it is a constant struggle. I have to work at it. It is not easy. It is a lifelong effort. It is a daily struggle. It is a Path we must carve out and walk each day. And if you think you've reached it, you've failed to understand that it is the pursuit and searching that is the Path; the value and worth is in the journey; not the reaching or attainment of a goal. You cannot reach Everest without climbing the mountain.

It is an endeavor worthy of a spiritual being inhabiting a physical body
That is what you are.

I am aware that I can fail through my humanity to be pure in my intent spiritually. But as we have said before, it is a noble and glorious struggle. It is a struggle that gives Meaning and Purpose to our lives. One that gives us Balance and Power in a frenzied world. Walk the Path and enjoy the journey.

Who Has What?

Do you have things...or do things have you?

4

WHO HAS WHAT?

Throughout human history, we have made it our habit to accumulate "things." There is a difference between having things you need and having things you just want. But it still isn't that simple. You need a house, but do you need a 1200 square foot house, or do you need a 5000 square foot house? Can you live in a 500 square foot house with four kids if you have to? Some would argue that you don't actually need a house at all; at least not in the conventional sense. I presume you could have a small tent or a giant tent. How about a vehicle? Can you survive with a small used economy car or truck, or do you want a brand-new state of the art machine? But do you actually need a vehicle at all? Could you survive with only having a bike? How about just a good durable pair of shoes? It would be very enlightening to wind down everything we say we need and determine what we really need and what we want. For many in today's rampant consumer culture, wants become needs, because you just have to have that handbag or watch or shoes.

I think the answer is that we likely need much less than we have in order to survive. Yet, we think we need things that we don't really need. One can argue that the insatiable human drive to want more, is what has built this civilization from a society of hardship and adversity, to a society of plenitude. From the beginning of humanity, we have collected things we didn't need. Some would say that it isn't just a bad habit, but instead a vice or addiction. In fact, for many, it is a vice and an addiction. Retail stores and on-line companies thrive on these addictions and are brutally effective with the methods they employ to exploit this part of the human condition. I was discussing this very subject with someone recently and we marveled at the innumerable things there are that one can buy. We have this unique need to possess all manner of physical things. We want to possess; we want to have; we want to own. It's mine! It's all mine!

I am reminded of a child who has a roomful of playthings which at first provided a fleeting and very temporary sense of joy and satisfaction. They just got tired of the novelty. The passing of time has faded the short-lived thrill. The toys lay in a heap, unused, not enjoyed and virtually devoid of any feeling to the child. It is as if the child doesn't know or care that they are there anymore. That is an unintended consequence of having too much. The appreciation is gone. Then a visitor comes over and brings a child, unknown to the child who has now lost interest in the toys. Well, these are all new toys to the visiting child, and they create excitement at first sight! Suddenly without invitation, he begins to play with these new-found toys. Now, something very strange but very human, happens. The "owner" of the old forgotten toys rears up and says, "Those are mine!", and moves to protect his property as if it were somehow newly valuable to him. What an astounding reaction! The entire concept of having and owning some "thing" manifested in a simple interaction between two children who would seem to be immune to the vices, habits and addictions of adults. We learn young. Or is it perhaps that it is not learned behavior, but human nature instead? What do you think?

It is difficult to explain this visceral and intense emotion, but it is real. Fast forward now as we move into adulthood and we have myriad examples of things we have or at least we think we have; houses, vacation homes, cars, golf clubs, bikes, TVs, gold, jewelry, art, wine collections, expensive watches, designer clothing; and the list goes on, ad nauseum. "I have a new Audi..." "Yeah, I just got a new Big Bertha driver..." "We just closed on our new home in a swanky neighborhood." "Did you see my new ring? It's two carats!" "I'll have the '76 Krug Cabernet Sauvignon." (Correction, it's no longer Cabernet Sauvignon, it's a "Cab"). "Yeah I'll have the Cab, or maybe the Pinot would be better." (Noir or Grigio?)

For many, the evidence of wealth is represented by numbers on a piece of paper, a statement of account or digits on a computer screen. How real is it? What is it really worth? We may find out someday, and the answer may not be pleasant. I recall my Father-in-law showing me his savings "passbook" from his bank showing what I then considered a huge amount of money. Those were the days when the bank teller wrote in the amount of your savings deposit and calculated the accrued interest so that you would have a current balance. I mentioned to him that he had lots of money. His response was so very enlightened for those times. Without hesitation, he said, "I don't have any money. It's just numbers on a piece of paper." It wasn't even dollars in his hands. It was numbers on a piece of paper. And yet, what do we want? We want bigger numbers on that piece of paper. It is never enough. The slavery of it is all too ironic. Recall our earlier discussion about Rockefeller and how it was never enough, and he just wanted a little bit more.

Yes, indeed we do have a lot of stuff and we want even more stuff. It is stunning to stop and think of all the things we have. Even more stunning is all the "stuff" we *can* have. A simple walk through a mall reveals a paradise of things you can have. It is all stuff we can have someday. So, we don't just have things, we have hopes and dreams for things we do not yet possess. We also have ideas we own and cherish, because after all, ideas are extremely personal and not to be stolen or misinterpreted. "Hey, that's *my* idea!"

Somehow, we "advanced" to the point where we owned everything that can be imagined; literally. The problem with having and owning all this stuff is that it becomes an obsession. We're hooked! It's just like a drug. We want more and more things. We can't stop wanting and we can't stop getting stuff.

Another problem is that we want to keep possessions. We do not want to leave them. When something is stolen from you, you feel "violated." It is a revealing word we use when something is taken from us. It is as if something intrinsic to us was ripped away. It was a part of you and now, no longer is. Something is missing. You have been violated.

It is interesting to note that Native American cultures do not recognize ownership of land. For them there is no deed of ownership or risk of foreclosure. The people own the land. Only recently have Native Americans had title to property. That was a result of integration into mainstream society which led to home ownership and lending requirements. So, now they can own their homes and property, and can also lose it to foreclosure. Yes, we are indeed an advanced culture.

How sad and tragic that possessions affect us in this way. You feel that you have lost Power, and you feel out of Balance. So, do we really have all of these things? Or...

Do things have us?

Think about that for a moment. Do you have things, or do they have you? It is definitely a difficult proposition to think of a life devoid of possessions. Understand, that I am not proposing that we not have possessions. Certainly, I do not promote a Spartan existence of pain, adversity, sacrifice that is unwilling, or paucity of the bare necessities to survive. But I do espouse a Spartan discipline of having the capacity and ability to decide to live without, if one were to so choose or if one was required to do so. Clearly, if it is in Balance, there is no reason to not have the benefit of our science, developments, comfort, efficiencies and civilization. What we lack is the discipline to "walk away" from them. ***To have peace without them.*** I am often struck by the seemingly sincere and passionate pronouncements by religious leaders of many faiths who encourage their adherents to tithe in a manner somehow conveniently prescribed by the teachings of their faith. Not to worry where the money goes or for what purpose it is used. "You will be rewarded 100 times!" 100 times 100!!! It is as if your heartfelt charitable gift is now calculated as an investment upon which you can depend will return a certain sum. There is an old saying: "Give without remembering; Take without forgetting." This theology of economics and prosperity, I believe, has warped our Purity of Intent when charitable giving is now considered an investment with a promised return on investment. That tax-free ten percent really adds up...

So, who has what?

Are we in fact "owned" by our own possessions?
Who has the Power?
What has the Power?
If you can release it without remorse, then you have the Power. If you cannot, then possessions have the Power over you.
Release your addiction to possessions, while still enjoying them in Balance.
Maintain Balance and Power in a world ruled by a frenzy to have possessions.

Release...

Have Peace and Strength.

"If you can make one heap of all your winnings
and risk it all on one turn of pitch and toss,
and lose,
and start again at your beginnings
and never breathe a word about your loss."

The Truth

It does not need our acknowledgement...
It simply exists

5

THE TRUTH

Aaaah! *The Truth*!! This is an elusive and nebulous concept for something that seems to be, and should be, so very absolute. In his inspiring writings in "A New Earth," Eckhart Tolle evokes thoughts seldom challenged. But it is in challenging the so-called Truth and conventional wisdom, that we get nearer to it. As we have already learned, conventional wisdom is many times not wisdom at all. It has been said that faith is the enemy of Truth because it keeps you from searching past faith to the Truth. Others say that if you have faith, that of itself is the Truth. Yet, the Truth exists as Truth regardless of what we may think it is versus what someone else may think it is. It exists on its own without need for confirmation. And of course, many people believe that their truth is the only truth, even though it may not be Truth at all. How many wars have been fought and millions killed in the name of Truth? One person's Truth is another person's heresy, hence the many wars that have afflicted our human race. Further, Truth is not only the realm of the mind, it is also the domain of politics and religion. Forget for a moment the Truth that is in your mind about politics and religion. There is likely a different reality of Truth that exists apart from those beliefs. Yet another problem is that people believe their own so-called facts. One would think that facts are transcendent; that they, like Truth, are independent of our beliefs and opinions. It has been said that "everyone is entitled to their own statistics." You can begin to see the problems with Faith, Facts and Truth.

We want the Truth to conform to our own ideas and beliefs

Imagine for a moment that you live in the middle ages, when people believed that the earth was flat. Well, it seems reasonable after all because to the naked eye, the Earth is flat. If you were to be situated from a high enough perspective, perhaps you may perceive a slight curvature in the Earth, but the brain, and even the mind, ignore the remote possibility because it was conventional "wisdom" that the Earth was flat. In fact, anyone who posited any "theory" to the contrary, was considered a heretic. The facts, beliefs and Truth did not match up. Never mind that the closest celestial bodies to the Earth, the Sun and the Moon, appear to at least be circular if not spherical. But the brain continued to ignore the possibility that the Earth was round because the Truth was that the Earth was flat; except for a few people who dared look past faith and belief, to seek Truth. It might surprise you to know that the Greek, Pythagoras, posited that the Earth is spherical almost 2,600 years ago! In fact, Eratosthenes calculated the circumference of the Earth 2,300 hundred years ago. Of course, that means he knew the Earth was a sphere and his calculation was off by a mere 46 miles!

Then slowly and grudgingly and mostly fearfully, because someone was willing to risk ridicule, punishment and being ostracized, an idea emerged, based on a foundation of many newly believed mini truths, that perhaps there was a new **paradigm**. The Earth must be round, (it's really slightly elliptical) or this system, the Solar System couldn't function. What were the elements that brought about the new way of thinking? Thinking about:

Night and Day;
Lunar Cycles;
Physical appearances;
Weather cycles;
Ocean tides;
The movement of the planets and stars;
Shadows
The Summer Solstice
Equinox

They were all clues, but someone had to be watching and thinking as Eratosthenes was, 1,800 years before Columbus sailed West. Then Columbus manifested his belief in the newfound Truth that the Earth was a sphere and sets sail into history and the rest as they say, "is history." Again, what is Truth? We can also say with confidence that the Truth was the Truth before Eratosthenes the Greek polymath calculated the circumference of the Earth to within a few miles *almost 2,300 years ago*!! It is commonly accepted that Columbus discovered America. It is also highly conjectured, based on some historical data which is also ostensibly factual, that several others preceded Columbus to the Americas. The difference is probably that Columbus and his successors stayed, conquered and settled South and Central America along with the southern regions of North America. Remember, it is always about Perspective.

My son David once asked me, "Dad, have you ever wondered what is right today, but was considered wrong 1000 years ago?" From the mouths of babes...comes so much wisdom and questions that are difficult to answer.

The world and global society are replete with such examples of so-called Truth. It would not be an exaggeration to say that there are as many truths or versions of the truth as there are persons living on this planet. It is amusing to listen to two divergent stories or accounts of events in a mediation or couples therapy session where each party has their version of the Truth. Most of the time these separate parties or persons are reasonable, well-meaning and honest. Yet it is striking how two points of view can be so shockingly different. Each party expresses their respective point of view as the representation of the Truth, is convinced of its veracity and believability and is puzzled and many times angered by the other party's view of the facts. So, are there several absolutes or at least more than one? Is there only one absolute?

When you calculate the viewpoints and perspectives of each person, it seems almost irrelevant that an "Ultimate Truth" exists. It seems that what is important to us in this consciousness is what we believe to be true; our Perception of the Truth. But the Ultimate Truth also exists, no matter that anyone even knows it exists, how it exists and why it exists. So, when Eratosthenes developed the calculation for the circumference of the Earth 2,300 years ago, did he discover something, or did he merely learn something? The circumference of the Earth was what it was, irrespective of anything Eratosthenes may have learned or calculated.

The truth that the Earth is spherical exists now and existed then, even though no one knew it or acknowledged it. We invent truths because we can. We are sentient and sapient beings. But many times, faith, belief, traditions, conditioning and so-called conventional wisdom are barriers to true knowledge and enlightenment. They do not set us free, but rather, imprison us and our minds in a very real mental prison. They keep us from discovering and acknowledging real truths.

So, can we hope to traverse this chasm? Can we open our minds to the possibility that there are Truths that are not apparent to us?

History as written, is often written by the conqueror. We read it in history books and treat it as factual, simply because it is written; and because it is written, it becomes fact. It is likely that there are many countless facts taught in history classes all over the world that don't faintly resemble the actual facts. The Truth of exactly how events unfolded and the precursor motivations whether political, economic or amorous in their basis, is many times written to serve an underlying motive. The Truth is not accounted for by persons with opposing perspectives. When two guys get into a fight, their stories about what happened are almost always different. In the United States of America, when one swears in court, the oath is to:

Tell the Truth,

The *whole* Truth, and

Nothing but the Truth.

It is a wisdom, seldom contemplated as to its comprehensiveness. We are thus instructed to simply tell the Truth; the facts as clearly and precisely as is possible in human thought and language.

We are also instructed to tell the *whole* Truth because while we may be reciting the Truth, omitting certain or any facts could prejudice the court's decision simply because not all the facts are available for proper discernment. Omission itself is as culpable as commission.

Finally, we are called to tell *nothing* but the Truth, because the inclusion of additional statements which may be personal opinions, or phrases that could color the view of the judge and jury, could also alter the understanding of the facts. In the U.S. court system, one is also under penalty of perjury if one does not comply with those highly specific instructions.

Does that guarantee that the Truth will be known or that justice will prevail? I submit to you that while it is a highly structured and pragmatic exercise, it does not ensure absolute Truth. My father used to say (in Spanish) "Cada cabeza es un mundo." Loosely translated it means, "In every mind there is a universe." The implication is that it is a "different" universe and therefore a different understanding and different laws that govern its existence and how each of us views the world. How very stunning and yet how very wonderful. But those sometimes-disparate views can result in minor nuances or vast differences in thinking, interpretation, understanding and ultimately in how people behave. And so, we attempt to transcend this issue with language, specificity and punctilious grammar and syntax. We are actually pretty good at it, but nonetheless we are thus prisoners of our words and their interpretation(s). In the past several decades, our empirical disciplines in science and discovery tell us that we have finally come to countless truths in fields from quantum mechanics to intelligent design, each attempting to move a theory forward in order to promote beliefs as fact. It is virtually guaranteed that these will not be final Truths or facts, but instead the foundations for yet more accurate Truths yet to be determined. It is safe to conjecture that we know very little of the vastness and types of Truths in the Eterniverse.

Consider for a moment that the entity that we call "God" is not at all what we have been taught to be the Truth. Consider that God, the Supreme Entity, the Universal Consciousness, is not a male or a female, but that it just "*IS*." It just exists in an eternal now. That "*IT*" is so great that "*IT*" cannot be described or even imagined by our minds and beyond comprehension. It is, in a word, ineffable.

Many believe by faith and by training that God is a Being that has certain characteristics, but these Truths are perhaps of our own design. And if that design is human, it unfairly limits that which is really God; that which cannot be described or defined. The Truth is that whatever God is, whatever form it has, however it exists, it is simply what it is, regardless of what we believe it to be or how we perceive it to exist.

Being raised a Catholic Christian, I believe in God. However, perhaps in contravention to dogma, I do not claim to know what *it* is or why *it* is; only that *it is*.

This is the basis of the Old Testament account of Moses, troubled by his God given responsibility to set His people free. When Moses asks, "He who has no name, Who shall I say sent me?" He who has no name replied, tell them 'I AM' sent you. (YHWH in Hebrew; the Tetragrammaton). What could be a more perfect description of God in human language?

I AM

I simply exist in this Universe.

I AM THE ETERNIVERSE

How powerful and how revealing. So, what is the Truth? In a very real and living way, the Truth is what we believe it to be. But the real Truth is independent of us. It is not aware of us and it does not change because of what we believe it to be. It simply is; it exists. We are blessed and fortunate if we seek it honestly and with Purity of Intent, unafraid of what we will learn and not burdened by centuries and eons of cultural and traditional indoctrination. This endeavor and the brave decision to pursue this search is what gives you Power. It permeates your body, soul and spirit and opens the gates to Enlightenment. The interesting thing is that even with this discipline of seeking the Truth, we can all arrive at different Truths.

I believe that someday, when our physical existence is completed on this Earth, we will know all Truth. We will not be encumbered by physical limitations including time and space. Our journey in this existence is to seek and experience that Enlightenment, if even only in glimpses before we transcend into the next existence. The Quintessential. That Fifth Element that is not of the physical, but of the spiritual realm.

WHAT IS RIGHT AND WHAT IS WRONG?

"Tell me not in mournful numbers,

Life is but an empty dream!

For the soul is dead, that slumbers,

And things are not what they seem."

Life is real! Life is earnest! And the grave is not its goal;

Dust thou art, to dust thou returnest,

Was not spoken of the soul....

But to act that each tomorrow, find us farther than today....

 Henry Wadsworth Long Fellow
From: The Psalm of Life
This is the beginning of this wonderful writing by Longfellow. The entire poem is included in the Appendix. At first reading, it seems to indicate an abandonment of all hope and positive expectation. But in reality, if one listens, the message is quite the opposite. It is a message of hope and a search for clarity of vision. For the reality is truly that things are not what they seem. We are reminded of some of our thoughts in the previous paragraphs about Truth and how we perceive things to be in our minds as opposed to how they may actually be, in fact. This can be called a willing suspension of disbelief, because it provides a comfortable platform upon which to rest our minds.

Longfellow's message, as one reads and understands the full message, is one of hope in the face of what appears to be Surrender to the tribulations of this life. Likewise, this can be applied to how we view things as Right or Wrong. I have often wondered why there are so many divergent views and opinions, indeed convictions, that things are right and wrong. Some things are right. They are acceptable. Some things are wrong. They are not acceptable. It is the dualism we need to identify opposites as we perceive them in this existence. It is merely language, the alliteration of vowels and consonants which make those two words the equivalent of right and wrong. What if we understood black to mean right, and white to mean wrong? What if we were conditioned to react to the color red as "Go" and green as "Stop?" Would it change the integral interpretation of what really is Right or Wrong or Stop and Go? What if we called Darkness "Day" and Sunlight "Night", or if left was right and right was left? Similarly, in this world of billions of people which equal billions of mental universes, there are myriad convictions of what is right and what is wrong. One is then led to the question, "who decided what is right and what is wrong?" Most religions will tell you that God decided what is right and what is wrong. Yet, there were things in the Old Testament that were right, that in the New testament are wrong. Did God change its mind? Or did humans get involved? I am not saying that either is right or wrong or that these rules and laws are not well intentioned. I am just asking the question.

Religion (not spirituality) is a prime example of this conflict. It can be argued that religion, politics and their accompanying dogmatic and fervent teachings are responsible for more wars, death, conflict and discord than any other institution(s). From the Crusades, a Christian undertaking and Jihad, a Muslim belief, to Stalin's and Mao's, political credos, we see entire populations mobilized and destroyed to defend and promote that which each respective group believes is the "Right", versus what is Wrong with the adversary.

These beliefs are so entrenched and conditioned into the brain that their proponents are literally prepared and willing to sacrifice their lives to defend the belief that they are on the "right side." In Christian dogma, Jesus Christ is sitting at the "right hand of the Father". Why do we greet each other with a right-handed handshake? In Roman times to enter a household with the left foot first or to greet your host with your left hand was considered an insult and was believed to bode ill will upon the household. In Latin, the left is "sinestra", which is the origin of our modern meaning of the word "sinister" or in other words "that which threatens something bad, dark or evil; dishonest or wicked." So, a greeting or entry with the left hand or foot respectively is widely considered to be wrong. How did this become so? Perhaps it is because 95% of the population is right-handed and 95% of the population steps forward with the right foot? Therefore, because of this physiological trait, right is acceptable, and left is sinister. In many cultures throughout history, left-handed people were viewed as evil outcasts. We can sure make up some weird stuff.

What if we didn't shake hands, but instead bowed our heads as many Eastern cultures do? How do our Asian brothers and sisters view this odd practice of shaking hands instead of simply bowing and not touching each other upon greeting each other? Right hand or left hand? It really doesn't matter. *Shaking hands may be the wrong thing to do, even if it is done with the right hand!!* It all seems so very confusing doesn't it? What is right to one, is wrong to another. In ancient cultures, a man could have many wives and concubine slaves. In fact, much of a man's wealth was determined by the number of wives and concubine slaves he possessed. In those days, such a position was not only approved of, it was respected and valued. Fast forward to modern society and Western civilization as we know it and accept it. Would such relationships be tolerated? Not only are current social mores in opposition to it, it is also illegal and punishable by imprisonment!!! That tradition and social custom has transformed from wealth and respect, to social pariah and prison! Of course, a virus can change the rules ever more.

Who decided which was right and which was wrong and why was it decided? And when did it change from right to wrong? If you would like a first-hand view of how we see things so differently, go to a court hearing during a trial where two parties are involved in a lawsuit. You will be struck by the passion each party exhibits in support of their respective "right vs. wrong" positions.

Well at least today, in large part, we are settling these disputes without guns and swords and duels. However, at the conclusion of the trial, one party feels wronged, but he knows he was right. In a more perfect world, they would Inquire and Listen, with Purity of Intent, outside of the court system, see the other mirror of themselves, Reconcile and shake hands, or maybe bow in respect.

So, what is right and what is wrong? Perhaps this dichotomy is best expressed in the Book of Ecclesiastes from the Old Testament. Right and wrong are accepted and rejected respectively by different peoples and societies at different times and different places depending on what serves the conventional thinking of the time, whether it be religions, political or societal.

To everything there is a Season,
 and a time to every purpose under the heaven:
A time to be born, and a time to die;
A time to plant, and a time to pluck up that which is planted;
A time to kill and a time to heal;
A time to break down and a time to build up;
A time to weep and a time to laugh;
A time to mourn and a time to dance;
A time to cast away stones and a time to gather stones together;
A time to embrace and a time to refrain from embracing;
A time to get and a time to lose;
A time to keep and a time to cast away;
A time to rend and a time to sew;
A time to keep silence and a time to speak;
A time to love and a time to hate;
A time of war and a time of peace.

"Ecclesiastes"

And so, it seems that right and wrong are present and alive in each person's conscience and mind's eye. Right and Wrong are also driven by Perspective, Conscience, Justification, personal benefit and perhaps even survival, further motivated by different eras of time and place. We should be mindful of the precious vintages and varietals of the differences cultivated by all of us across time and place, even if we may be on the wrong side of things.

While not surrendering our conviction in our belief in what is right and what is wrong, understanding that there exists another universe, if not innumerable universes of right and wrong, gives us Enlightenment.

Balance and Power;
Thoughtfulness;
Patience;
Discernment;
Peace and Strength.

Body Brain and Mind Spirit

This is the mind and body problem

6

BODY BRAIN AND MIND SPIRIT

Memento Mori.... Remember, we must all die. (Latin)

The Latin quote and reference are obviously referring to the physical realm. We want to discuss that nebulous connection between the Mind/Spirit which I posit exists in eternity, past and future, as a form of energy; and Body/ Brain, which because it is by definition a physical organism, is also therefore temporal. The Brain has a physical beginning and a physical end, unlike the Spirit.

What is it about dying and death that dominates our thinking and our lives so much? It is inevitable that people die all around us all the time and we become both numb and attentive to it all at once. The dichotomy is that those subjects dominate our thoughts while at the same time we seem to want to maintain a distance from them if only in our minds and thoughts. The great escape from this physical and temporal life has been a source of puzzlement and wonderment to us for thousands of years. The Egyptians had their obsession with preservation of the mummified body, the afterlife and pyramids as "eternal" tombs. Today, pageantry and ceremony rule the day. A grand celebration at birth and an even "grander" event at death. Today, the great majority of all dollars spent on health care are spent in the last days of a person's life in anticipation of the inevitable. After death, some cultures bury the dead as quickly as possible while others prolong the process. The Greeks would place coins over the eyes of the deceased so that the person, now traveling into the next life would have passenger fare to pay for the crossing of the river Styx, which the boatman Charon would gladly accept as payment. I don't believe there is any mention of what Charon would do with so many fares having been paid to him in a place with no place to shop in the underworld.

Some cultures bury their dead, some traditions call for the burning of the dead in funeral pyres while others built pyramids and other ostentatious buildings to celebrate the deceased while ostensibly sending them to the next life, however misunderstood or unknown that concept may have been then. I believe it is still misunderstood and unknown today.

But it wasn't just death that was being celebrated. In many cultures it was a recognition and desire of existence in some form after physical death, though the proposed and believed form of existence was a human construct. No one wants to think that when we die it is unequivocally over! The concept of existing in this physical realm, then not existing at all in any form is difficult to accept. All of these forms of dealing with death have a basis in some historical context of tradition, culture, necessity or other influencers such as religion, simple and sincere spirituality or perhaps the thought that our consciousness would survive in some form forever; for all eternity, whatever that is. After all, the Eterniverse doesn't keep track of Time or Space. The Eterniverse doesn't know or care that it is 2:00 PM or that it is Sunday morning, or October 31, that we are 4.24 light years distant from Proxima Centauri or that the Earth orbits the Sun every 365.24219878 days.

It is now known (if anything is actually really known) that Neanderthals buried their dead. Some 100,000 plus years ago, relatives of our ancestors that we thought were primitive "cavemen", unthinking brutish creatures of subhuman intelligence, were burying their departed brethren. That is not what we would expect from cavemen that we have believed were more akin to apes than humans. Yet, here were these quasi primitive looking, but thinking beings that had it in their Minds that there was enough value in the living that there should be a ceremony upon death and remembrance of the departed. They exhibited value in their lives, culture and tradition. Why would they bury their departed? Why would a being such as a Neanderthal have such a belief? What is the underlying thought process that manifests itself in recognition of life and existence being of such importance?

The answer lies in consciousness and awareness of self. We have named ourselves "Human Beings". What does the word "being" mean to you? I am being picky; you are being strong; It is a state of existence. What does it mean to "be"? (Note: In Spanish the term for Human Being is "Ser Humano". This is interesting because the infinitive "to be" can be said two ways in Spanish. "Ser" and "Estar". "Estar" signifies temporariness while "Ser" signifies permanence.) What does it mean when you say or think, "I Am"? I think, therefore I Am. If I am, and I know that I am, I also now need to know who I am, what I am, why I am and what my purpose for being might be. That capacity in a Mind and not in the physical brain is a source of inquiry and wonder. Can a solely physical being with a Brain, but with no Mind, have such thoughts? Or is a Mind, which is apart from and not solely a part of the Body, a necessity to have such questions about existence?

I have long thought that the Four God Keys are Consciousness, Spirit, Soul and Mind. Perhaps they are simply different names for the same thing. But these Four God Keys are not a part of the body, but instead are apart from the physical body and brain. That is what makes this discussion of the Body Brain and the Spirit Mind so very intriguing. Think for a moment about these Four God Keys. Your Consciousness makes you aware of self and it also makes you aware of a Conscience and the whole idea of what is right and what is wrong. Again, when does the knowledge of right and wrong start? Some people argue that we are born with the knowledge of good and evil. Does an infant know the difference between right and wrong? The whole idea of right and wrong and if it is nature or nurture, is a subject unto itself and is the topic for another writing. If you believe in Spirit, you can then believe that a Spirit, your Spirit, has existed eternally in the past and that your Spirit simply inhabits your temporal physical body until it moves into the next dimension or eternal number of dimensions. Your Spirit had to experience this physical realm as part of its path without which it would have been incomplete. Your Spirit needed this physical life.

For many, the Soul is a manifestation of a sort of conduit that leads to a different realm. The Mind would seem to be a manifestation of the physical brain as an organ, but the Mind conjures intangible thoughts and emotions and feelings, experiences and nonverbal and nonphysical manifestations of existence. After all, what is a thought, where does a thought come from and in what form does a thought exist? Is a thought pure energy? If it is pure energy, can it be measured as energy like electromagnetism is measured and identified? Is the Mind a part of the Body and Brain? This is an age-old conundrum. If they in fact are apart from each other, how can the Body Brain die, and the Spirit Mind die with it? Perhaps it is because the Mind and Body are connected by an Energy Stream, and when physical Death occurs, the Mind continues to live in "No Time". What is No Time? It is Now, and Now is eternal. It never ends. In the "Now", the past and future are nonexistent. There is no Time or Space to keep you prisoner.

One question that is sure to come up is "are you afraid of dying and death"? Most brave souls say "no", even though they may in fact fear death. Young people don't fear death because they don't think they are going to die, at least not for a long time. Older people don't fear death because they may have had enough of life, are tired of this life and are prepared to leave this physical existence. But the thought is omnipresent. Why is death always on our minds?

For some people death is more present than life.

Some are more fearful of life than of death.

I have heard people say many times "if I ever die..." So, in a way, we subconsciously put it off as if it will never happen. Yet entire industries are built around dying, death, preparation for death and the ceremony that occurs when we die. Then there is the handling of the "remains", which I always thought was a strange term for a dead body. How about "personal effects?" That's a good one too.

Was it always so? Did ancient beings have the same attention to death as we do? Was there a time in the primordial past when hominids didn't bother to bury the dead? As we have discussed before, anthropologists and archeologists will say that they can reasonably evidence dates and times in the distant unrecorded past when hominids did in fact start to care about death and started thinking about what happened to the spirit of the person after death. There seems to have been and continues to be, an innate desire or need to believe that we will continue to exist in another realm or dimension, lest what reason would there be to have lived at all? For what purpose were we placed here? Indeed, why were we born at all?

In the grand scope of Time and Space, it is hard to ignore that our lives are so very miniscule as compared to Time and Space. Only because we think about periods of time in seconds, minutes, hours, weeks, months, years and decades, and distance in feet, yards, miles and light years do we become bound by that which we believe to be "Time" and "Space". Why do we measure Time and Space? We measure them because we want to control them somehow. Yet Time and Space are not calculable in reality. Again, the Eterniverse doesn't know what time it is or how far light travels in time. Time and Space are irrelevant to the Eterniverse. It is for this very same reason that distance too, is irrelevant to the Eterniverse. Yet we spend billions trying to measure both as if by being able to measure them, we can somehow control them. So, what happens to time when your physical Body Brain dies? Similarly, where do you exist, if anywhere, when your physical Body Brain dies? Why would you exist here in this physical realm if only to die and have no remaining, surviving and living Spirit Mind with no purpose?

We should also now ponder the issue of Eternity. I have written in my book "Entheos, God Within", (Vitam Aeternum), that Eternity is a human construct. Again, the Eterniverse does not know or care about Eternity. The only thing that exists is "Now", and even that is so instantaneous that it too can barely be recognized as existing because it is gone before you can grasp it. But if you can think about it for a moment you can grasp the idea that "Now" is eternal. Now never ends. Think about that for a moment. ***Now never ends. So, if Now never ends, it is the thing that doesn't end and always exists and will never stop existing. The idea is that "right now" is as eternal as it gets. So, if we are to grasp that idea, we can infer that we are living in Eternity at this very second.***

It is Eternow

"Now" is an instantaneous transformation of all things and all events in the Eterniverse. That instantaneous transformation includes the Body, Brain and Mind Convergence upon physical death.

But what does all that have to do with death, the Body Brain and the Spirit Mind?

What then is death really? If the Body and Mind are distinct, how exactly can these two forms of existence interact and co-exist, especially if they exist in different dimensions, one physical and the other non-physical? Is the Mind, Consciousness of itself? Are the Physical Body and Brain apart from the Mind, Consciousness and self-awareness?

Perhaps using the term "Human Mind" is anathema and presumptive as the Human may have nothing to do with the Mind in the physical realm. Descartes wrote, "Cogito ergo sum", (I think, therefore I Am). This raises the idea and question of the distinct realms of Mind and Matter and how they are distinct and apart in one manner and connected somehow in another.

The Mind is not governed by the laws of physics.

Is there an empirically identifiable point of contact between the Mind and the Body Brain? I propose that the continuous transformation of the "Now" is a Mind Stream. First, dying is a human construct. It is an element of existence that, like all things human, requires definition therefore we provide a definition. It is something that happens with everyone and everything. It is a constant in this physical dimension. We are dying from the moment of conception. Therefore, in a very real way, ***we are living and dying at the same time*** in an eternal "Now". Physical and final body death is just the last manifestation of this physical "Now" existence.

That begs the question, "Did you exist in some manner before your physical life began?" We can get to that question later as we discuss the Mind. For many people the ontological question is a more profound, but more difficult one; "Why do I exist?" If you are religious or spiritual you would ask, "Why is God" and "How is God?" Depart for a moment from the dogma and religious training you have had in your life. Ask...why would God exist?

If you believe that your Spirit existed in some manner before your physical life began, shall we then ask, "Why do I exist now and why did I exist in eternity past?" What is the purpose of having lived in Eternity and now existing in a physical body? What was seeking what? And why was it seeking it? Was my Eternal Spirit seeking a physical and temporal body for some reason? What could be the reason for my Spirit seeking to inhabit a physical body? Perhaps it is because the Mind and Body experience and connection is a necessary phase or step in the ascendance of existence. Or perhaps it is a humorous transmogrification to entertain the gods.

It has been said that death and God are mutually exclusive. That if there is a God, death cannot exist with God in the equation. I submit to you the exact opposite. That physical death and God are inextricably intertwined. That the moment of physical death and the simultaneous spiritual transcendence is itself the manifestation of God's presence. One cannot exist without the other being; that physical death triggers the embrace of God, Mind and Body. How could it be otherwise? Think about death without God being present. It would seem to be an abandonment and very difficult to reconcile. Because physical death is merely a transformation, the Mind and Spirit continue to exist in the God entity; in the Eterniverse. We must recognize that Power as existing in a very real sense. It can then be argued and posited that Death in the human sense does not really exist. It is a mirage. The transformation is seamless. When and how does one know that he or she has "died?"

Let us perform, in private, a very simple test to demonstrate this seamless occurrence in this physical world as we pass to the next dimension.

Place your hands together in the form of prayer, palm to palm;
Place your thumbs on your chin or the bottom of your chin, and the outside of your forefingers on the tip of your nose;
Feel every part of your hands as they touch the other hand and your hands as they touch your chin and nose;
Isolate your fingers and feel how they meet each other;

Now isolate your forefingers and feel how they individually meet with your nose;

Now, see which of your forefingers, the right one or the left one, you can actually feel. You are feeling both fingers. You actually can't separate them. Where does one start and the other end? You should be able to feel them separately because they are separate digits, but you can't separate the feeling in them.

You can do the same exercise with any other part of your hands and face, and you will have the same result.

This is how Life and Death are connected. Inextricably intertwined.

It is interesting that science has discovered that upon the death of the body, approximately 1000 genes survive the body's death and display an elevated level of activity for several days after the death of the body when it is a non-living cadaver. Why only 1000 genes and why do they come to life upon death of the body? What could be the reason for this to occur? Indeed, what could be the reason? What transformation might be occurring that we can only surmise? At the quantum level, something is occurring.

When I was in Catholic school as a young man, I had the good fortune of being a top student in a top-rated parochial school. That opened the door for the nuns to request that I serve funeral masses since I was not going to get behind on schoolwork. I gladly did my duty as an altar boy. Learning Latin was an unexpected benefit.

At the funerals I witnessed unending and abject sorrow, wailing, desperation of loss, despair and every deep emotion a person can have at such a time. I internalized these intense feelings on a regular basis. I was impressed by how very differently people acted and reacted to the fact of physical death and departure of the body from this physical realm. Of course, there were the repeated statements of consolation where the loved ones would state that the deceased was in the arms of God, in a better place, was in eternal happiness, in heaven, at peace, eternal rest, with the angels, in paradise and all manner of commentary about how they should take heart in the current state of the deceased now being in paradise. All those ideas were based in some form of belief system that somehow life continued in some form of existence. We do not want to consider that we will stop living or existing after physical death. Is it consolation more for the deceased or more so a hope for the living?

I became very comfortable in the presence of death, the process of burying the dead, the ceremony and idea of death and I believed that in some way my presence served as solace to the family of the deceased. Later I realized that I was not at all uncomfortable being with someone when they were dying and who then actually died in my presence. In fact, I developed a wonderful exchange in this evolution. I gave the dying comfort and they gave me their Power. I believe the exchange to be very mutually beneficial, but I believe that I receive the better part of the deal. This is not morbid or dark. It is a very real thing in my life. I have witnessed several people including my Father (in my book Entheos, God Within, in the chapter entitled "Gathaspa"), my mother, Luciana and close friends and family passing from this life and I couldn't help but think about how exactly, a person with a "Mind" could be entirely dead. What happened to their thoughts? Where do they exist now? In what form do they exist? Are their thoughts a manifestation of their essence? Do they continue to exist in me? It is an answer that awaits us. Still, if there is existence after physical death, why would there be no evidence of it? Faith is not evidence. It is Faith, not fact. Can we know something we cannot see? Can you see gravity? Can you see electromagnetism (microwaves, Wi-Fi, etc.)? You can't see those forms of energy; however, you can witness the physical manifestations of those forms of invisible and intangible energies. A rock falls down, not up. Somehow, the microwave heats food. In a sense, because you see the physical manifestations of those energies, you no longer require Faith. Faith is no longer necessary when you have Fact. Can you see the Mind and Spirit? What might be the physical manifestation of those energies? I have known love and have known people whose love transcended this life, yet there seems to be a disconnect once someone dies. But the disconnect is physical, not spiritual.

But it made me think further. It made me think past the horizons of religious training and dogma. It made me think deeply about the Brain that exists in our bodies and how that physical organ we call a Brain has certain qualities that transcend physical life in connection with the Mind, yet I cannot express how that happens. But I believe that it does. Faith versus Fact.

Think about the Brain and its unfathomable complexities. Each Brain contains trillions of cells, and each cell contains 60 to 100 trillion atoms. It is an Eterniverse unto itself. Now think about the Mind and how it interacts with a human body. How does the Mind, being apart from the body, communicate with the body? How can a person have a Brain in their body and apart from that, have a Mind that is independent of that Brain? Surely when the physical body dies, the physical Brain dies with it.

But what of the Mind? Indeed, what of the Mind?

That is the thought that I couldn't escape. The question of the nonphysical realm of existence of the Mind, Spirit, Consciousness and Soul of which we seem to be aware in this physical realm. Somehow, these nonphysical elements communicate with the physical Brain in a form of energy the ancients called an energy stream. Yet, many philosophers and most scientists believe that the Mind is a manifestation of the Brain, and that they exist together in a kind of physical manner that is inseparable. Synapses and relays. All the scientific stuff. Let's explore further.

When an infant is born, does that infant's Brain come with a Mind? An infant does not have complex thoughts of which we are aware. Most have no cognitive recollection of being an infant. Can an infant have an idea or a thought? When does a child start having emotions or feelings such as fear, jealousy, hate, distrust, fear of loss, loneliness, envy, greed, regret, hope, loss of hope, anger, joy, love and despair? Fear is more primal and appears earlier, but even the emotion of fear itself is a nonphysical event. It is not tangible. What about Conscience and moral responsibility in an infant? Are Conscience and moral responsibility an inculcation of culture, tradition, conditioning and training or do they exist independent of those influencers? Is an infant born with an innate sense of moral responsibility? Does the Brain, independent of the Mind, and as an element of its physical existence, recognize and know morality and ethical behavior? What about those emotions and thoughts that seem to evolve such as those mentioned above?

Is a child born with Consciousness? Is a child born with a Conscience? Is an infant aware of itself and its own existence in the physical plane? Does a child know that it exists? When does a child come to know that something is right and that something is wrong? Does an infant have an inherent conscience, or is conscience a manifestation of the interpretation of the conditioning of society, and society's (and religion's) traditions, culture and teachings?

Others believe that the Mind (as opposed to the physical brain) is tantamount to a Spirit and to a Soul. It conjures thoughts, ideas, emotions and all manner of nonphysical elements that somehow co-exist with the physical realm. But if the Mind is a part of the Body, does it have a physical manifestation? How can a nonphysical entity communicate with and cause a physical manifestation in a physical Body? If your Mind has a thought that no other human has thought, what happens to that thought when the physical body dies? Does it continue to exist? Is that thought out there in the Eterniverse? Has that thought always existed and been realized by you only today? How can that thought die with the Body if the thought is not physical?

Another conundrum arises when one attributes Responsibility, Free Will and Conscience to the Mind, such that it then renders the Body (the human being) not responsible for its own acts, since the Mind governs the Body's behavior, and they are separate and apart from the other. The discussion continues with the connection of the immaterial Mind to the material Body/Brain. But even neuropsychology, neuropsychiatry and neurophilosophy only state that the Mind is an "**Undefined Property**". What exactly could that mean? Again, shall we ask, "Does a thought exist"? In what form does a thought exist? If it is energy, can it be measured? If the energy can be measured, is it then also in the physical realm? Because thoughts cannot be seen, it does not mean they do not exist. Does a thought have substance?

What does existence mean if a thought does not exist? A thought exists by default.

If one is aware of it, or even if you are not aware of it, like anything else, it must exist somehow albeit in a manner that we may not yet understand. How then does a thought borne of the Mind continue to exist in the absence of the physical body?

Think again about gravity. We know it exists because it manifests itself in a physical reaction. However, you cannot see gravity. You can only see its manifestation. Yet we can see that gravity exists. The speed of light is not seen yet it exists. It is both tangible and intangible. There it is again; that nebulous connection between the physical realm and the Mind.

In Buddhism, *the Mind is a manifestation of thought, moment to moment, one thought moment at a time, making up a fast-flowing stream.* The Body/Brain is empty of Consciousness and of itself cannot access abstract existence and thought, i.e., it cannot access the Mind. Could one have a Mind without a Brain? If the Brain is physical, it dies. If the Mind is eternal Spirit, it has always existed. Therefore, yes, a Mind can and does exist without the physical Brain. But what of the experience of transplant donors who experience memories and other feelings of the donor? What is the connection of a donor of a physical organ and an abstract feeling by the organ recipient of a connection of Mind and Spirit, Soul and Consciousness? What does re-incarnation argue for? Is it a decision made by a Spirit to re-inhabit a human form to complete its journey; its Path; its Táo?

Are the Mind and Body connected only during life, then separated at death? I suggest that the Mind and Body are separate (yet somehow connected) during life and connect permanently at death to open the gates to the eternal Now in an instantaneous transformation from physical to spiritual, which of course exists in the Now.

Aristotle said, "It is not necessary to ask if the Body and Soul are one, just as it is not necessary to ask if the wax and its shape are one."

Perhaps it is the God element, the God Keys that tie, then unite these two very disparate yet connected realms of existence; the physical and the nonphysical and "spiritual" realms. Perhaps these Energy Streams, gravity, laws of nature, the Mind and Spirit and the "Now" are all manifestations of the God entity.

I have had far too many experiences that are not bound by Time and Space to not believe that somehow, someway, in a manner not understood by us, there exists another realm of energy or perhaps an Eterniverse of energies that constitute what we think of as eternity in Time and Space, even though it is surely a human construct. So, what does this mean to you and to your life here and now?

Seek and see the existence that is not manifested by physical death. Look past the pageantry and pomp and ceremony. Seek and find the Power of the Mind and Consciousness that has always existed and will always exist in you and others.

Ancient sages asked questions not so much because they believed there was an answer. They asked questions because the inquiry was the essence of Meaning and Purpose. Imagine for a moment that you knew chapter and verse, the Meaning and Purpose of your life. I submit to you that knowing every chapter and verse of your life in advance would subvert the true Meaning and Purpose of your life; that the search, the inquiry, the not knowing, the unpredictability, is the essence of Purpose and Meaning. The matrix of understanding and enlightenment is born out of these. Embrace the Inquiry. Do not fear what answer or enlightenment may come to you.

Find your Balance and Power.

Be Undefeatable.

Knowledge and Wisdom

All good things together came to me in Her company

7

KNOWLEDGE AND WISDOM

Knowledge would seem to be solely a function of the physical Brain as it functions in a highly complex manner to learn and remember things as acquired knowledge. Like a computer, all the connections, wires, synapses, electricity and physical networking yields a physical result; knowledge and information is stored and available for retrieval. On the other hand, Wisdom seems to correlate to the intangible nature of the Mind because I believe that Wisdom does not reside in the physical Brain. Problem solving, such as in a mathematical equation like Einstein's theory of relativity, is a function of the Brain, while Discernment which yields Wisdom, is a product of the Mind, yet Discernment cannot occur without the Brain assisting in the resolution and decision-making process. (Discern; from Latin. "cernire". To sift.)

What then, does it mean to think? Have you ever stopped to think about something? Anything? Everything? Clearly, we need a Brain to think. But consider this; a thought that you are having right now is not a tangible thing. You can't feel it or touch it with your hands. And even though you can't touch it and it is not a physical thing, you know that it exists. How is it possible that you can know that something exists even though you cannot evidence it physically? You can tell someone that you have a thought and even though you know that you are experiencing that thought, they cannot know it with certainty because they can't see or feel it. But you can. Here is the very strange bridge between the physical Brain and the intangible Mind. Your private intangible thought that no one else knows or understands *can* be manifested into a physical reality. For instance, an artist can have an intangible idea and image that becomes a priceless work of art once the artist physically paints the thought into visual reality on canvas. A musician who has a symphony in her thoughts can somehow magically reduce those thoughts into written musical notes for each instrument that can be read by a musician, and by doing so, creates an incredible piece of music that is heard in the auditory realm. The person with the thought writes the musical notes on a chart and those images mean something to the musician. The musician then takes those notes, which are but a written manifestation of her thoughts, then knows what strings or keys to play to create the sounds. If you think about it, it really is a miracle we can do this.

Many people have ideas and thoughts about new technology or products.

Many times, they will invest time in developing these thoughts into something that they imagine as a working and functional creation that can be useful in the world. The phone, television, electric light bulb, the automobile, electric motor, airplane, space shuttle, lasers, cellphone, computer and other similar devices started as a person's thought, and through a series of proofs of concept, purposeful or not, intended or not, a physical creation emerges. An interesting thing is that many of those people who have those brilliant thoughts are unable to make the transition from thought/idea to a working and functional physical product in the real world. Patents for products, processes and other intellectual property are a testament to the confluence of brilliant thoughts and the eventual creation of a functioning physical product or device. This is indeed an interesting connection between someone's thoughts and another person's ability to create something from the thoughts communicated to them.

Let's return to the concepts of Knowledge and Wisdom; (Problem Solving and Discernment). These disciplines and states of being, respectively, seem to be inextricable as if one can only exist alongside the other. Can you have Knowledge, but not Wisdom? Can abundant Knowledge and extensive experience be a contributor to Wisdom? Can you have Wisdom but not Knowledge?

What exactly is Knowledge? What do we really know? Five hundred years ago, we knew the Earth was flat. Now we know that the Earth is a sphere. What do we know today that will be refuted as untrue in the future?

There is also the question of Knowledge and Understanding. Imagine for a moment that you could memorize the Bible in its entirety. It sounds impossible when you can't remember your own cell phone number. Well, believe it or not there are people in this world who can. Some people have memorized the entire Bible and various other monumental writings!!! They are called **mnemonists**. If you asked this person a question about the Bible, they could quote chapter and verse with total accuracy and specificity. No errors, just facts. Such a person definitely has complete memorized recall and command of each and every word that is contained in the Bible. Such a person, it could be argued, has knowledge of the Biblical texts. But even in this very stark example, we can readily argue that the mnemonist may have knowledge in the form of recall of the text (the written words) but may not have knowledge of the message in the Bible or an Understanding of its content and intent. Of course, that makes a large assumption as to what the message really is, and we have hundreds of branches of Christianity to prove it, all proclaiming a unique and sometimes personal translation of the message. So, even with the idea of the ability of the physical Brain to learn, retain and retrieve information which we refer to as Knowledge, we are still subject to the nonphysical interpretation which is of the Mind and not of the Brain. We have the physical knowledge of the actual words; however, being able to recite words does not convey understanding of the words to that person.

What was really meant by those writings and the writings of other religions, politicians or philosophers? This transition from actual words into interpretation of the words and their meanings, transcends to the concept of the Mind. They are related, but very much different. In the movie, The Ten Commandments, Moses says that he encountered "He who has no name, The light of Eternal Mind." Surely this Supreme "Mind" would transcend any mere human Brain. I submit to you that they may in fact be one and the same.

Scientists tell us that when our physical bodies die, the Brain also dies with it, and indeed it does. It is a physical organ that can be seen, felt, dissected, preserved and observed. But we can't see the Mind. It does not manifest itself physically in a direct sense. Does the Mind also die, or does the Mind as Spirit and Soul continue to live?

Do you have a good Brain, or do you have a good Mind? Which would you rather have? There is no doubt that in this form of existence, in this reality, we cannot think without a physical Brain. At least that is the conventional "Wisdom." We think that other living creatures that have brains much smaller than humans, don't think and are not self-aware, at least as we know it. We use the word or term "animal instincts" to explain animal behavior. I'm not so sure we've got it right since we now "know" that some primates, dolphins, whales and other animals have some cognitive abilities.

Think for a moment that when a tsunami, volcano eruption or earthquake are imminent, all forms of living creatures behave in very curious, if not highly intelligent ways well before the event. They go to higher ground, seek refuge or do such other things to respond to the event, before it happens! The only creatures that don't react in that manner are Big Brained Homo Sapiens. We certainly have the bigger Brain, but we can't "see or feel" the event in advance like animals do. If it is the Brain that provides knowledge, why can't we know that such an event is about to occur. It is true that we have begun to harness science to predict and react to those natural phenomena, but it doesn't come naturally to us. It does come naturally to non-human creatures. How can that be possible? We should consider that there are different dimensions of knowing that we do not understand.

Maybe they have a certain "Mind Power" instead of Brain Power that gives them "Knowledge" of the event in advance. I am reminded of a test that was conducted along these lines that demonstrated this phenomenon.

In the test, the dog and the dog's owner were separated. The dog remained at home, while the owner traveled on business a thousand miles away. The dog was alone but was fed and given water by a caretaker. There was also a camera tracking the dog's movements, activities and moods. Mostly, the dog was bored, listless, lonely and inactive. But then something interesting happened. When the owner decided to come home and started packing in preparation somehow it seems the dog sensed his owner was returning and the cameras picked up the animal's excitement. How is this possible in our physical understanding, in this time and place? It has been argued that animals have a heightened sense of smell and hearing to compensate for their smaller brain and inability to think. Can a dog smell and hear 1000 miles away? Or is it something altogether different and transcendent? A different kind of Mind, and a different kind of reality that we don't comprehend, yet it exists; an energy stream. A dog can't invent or conceive of a computer, much less use one. And conversely, we can't feel things in the highly evolved manner they do. At least not all the time. I do believe we have glimpses into that dimension of thought and feeling, but they are fleeting. Perhaps we are evolving in a positive manner. Perhaps not.

I believe that humanity is at the crossroads of Enlightenment or annihilation. As you observe all the mayhem around you, it seems that we are in a race to see which occurs first. The argument for destruction is all around us. From viruses, eternal wars and conflicts to abuse of our natural resources. All the forces are aligned to set off a chain of events which could be irreversible. On the other hand, we see enormous and undeniable positive energies that can elevate us to a new level of Enlightenment; a new age of vision and purpose that transforms us into more evolved and spiritual beings. A world where character trumps capital; honesty defeats horror; fortitude overpowers fear; and where peace overcomes poverty. Purity of Intent in this pursuit would guide us on the right Path. Which will it be? Light or Darkness? Can we develop our Brains and Minds to transcend destruction?

Since the Neolithic period, we as humans have inexorably advanced and developed our Brain Power in a manner that is unparalleled. We have gone from flaking stones for use as cutting tools, to a trillion computer calculations per second, all in a few thousand years. Its incomprehensible how accelerated this evolution has been. Perhaps it is now time to learn to develop our Mind Power and not solely our Brain Power. As we vector into this crossroads, we will need our Minds more than our Brains. We will have to seek Discernment, Wisdom and Balance. Then we will be transformed into truly Powerful beings for the betterment of the Earth and the Eterniverse.

Wisdom

In the New American Bible, there is a Book called the Book of Wisdom, which does not appear in the King James and other versions of the Bible. In the Book of Wisdom, Solomon refers to Wisdom as "she" and "her". It is beautiful and it seems correct and appropriate. I have known and worked with many talented, smart, educated, insightful and wise men in my life. Many of whom I admire and respect. Some of whom I have chosen to emulate for their Strength, Balance, Power and Wisdom. They seemed to have a very special way of "seeing", like Black Elk of the Lakota Sioux.
Black Elk was a seer, wise man and spiritual leader. This is one of his writings.

ENLIGHTENMENT

Then I was standing on the highest mountain of them all,

Then round about me was the whole hoop of the world.

And while I stood there, I saw more than I could tell,

And I understood more than I saw,

For I was seeing in a sacred manner

The shape of all things in the spirit

And the shape of all shapes

As they must live together

LIKE ONE BEING.

The men I am referring to were calm, strong, discerning and focused in their views. They seemed to have Wisdom. But for all of these special men I knew, and there were only a few, they all seemed to have had to develop this Wisdom over time. They seemed to have had to work at it.

I mention this, because as compared to men, women seem to be blessed with Wisdom in abundance and without effort as an innate and natural gift. Over the centuries, due to sexist, political, religious and other motivations, women have been far less formally educated than men. Social rules and traditions valued their domestic contributions over their mental contributions. So, perhaps their Brains were not formally educated but their powerful Minds certainly seem to have compensated and our world is better because of it.

I am always impressed at the Wisdom of most women. They seem to have a certain "feel" for issues of character and trust, and what will work and what won't. They are thoughtful, careful and discerning. Men, on the other hand, seem more impetuous and will just rush into things even if they know little about it. Women contemplate. This difference and balance between the thoughtfulness of women and the aggression of men is likely what helped us survive and grow as a species. I say this in the most respectful manner possible, but can you imagine a woman starting a nuclear holocaust? Well, I'm sure there are some men who think a woman is capable of doing so.

I have a theory that the reason we live in homes, have domesticated plants and animals, plenty to eat, great works of art, epic writings, monumental buildings and great cities and civilizations, is because women saw the wisdom in growing and harvesting food (both plants and animals) in the same location year after year, and not having to move their camp every two weeks, and not freezing because they could stay inside a permanent residence. Then there was more time to think, paint, develop speech, develop writing in the forms of hieroglyphics and cuneiform and as a result the Brain grew and started having complex thoughts and problem-solving capabilities. Speacialization of trades followed one could then argue that the Brain developed in humans as a direct result of the Mind of women. Isn't it interesting that eastern faiths espouse being Mindful and not Brainful?

Of course, the exquisite combination of both Brain and Mind, and Man and Woman. has led to an equally breathtaking development of *Homo Sapiens Sapiens*. That's us, trying to stay alive; trying to stay in Balance. Working our way through these "once in an Eternity" lives we have and are experiencing.

Trying to figure it all out. Discernment. As mentioned before, the word comes from the Latin "cernire" which means to "sift...through." It makes sense, doesn't it? Discernment is the process of sifting through things to arrive at a well-reasoned, disciplined and Balanced decision.

Discernment is a basis for Wisdom. What is difficult to comprehend is whether the process of Discernment is conscious or unconscious. Is it innate or is it learned? Is it pragmatic or is it instinctive? Is it planned or unplanned? Is it the Brain or is it the Mind? One thing is for sure however, in matters of love, passion, envy, hate, greed, and all the so called " Seven Deadly Sins," it is the Mind that goes awry, and the Brain is a lonely orphan. That is a not so subtle reference to the old saying, " Success has many fathers and Failure is a lonely orphan." How does it all fit together? How do we glean and harvest the best that both Mind and Brain have to offer us? How do we maintain Balance between the two and enjoy the Power of both? I think it has much to do with making the effort to be aware that the Brain you have is the factory and fuel in the equation; the Mind is the realm of elevated thoughts and consciousness; while understanding that the energy stream between them is the lubricant that gives us this unique experience. To keep it Balanced we must let them be like nuclear fission, then fusion. Both merging and separate. What a glorious and wondrous event! What a mystery...

The merging of

Body and Soul;

Heaven and Earth;

Life and Death;

Divinity and Humanity

That Which Is Unseen

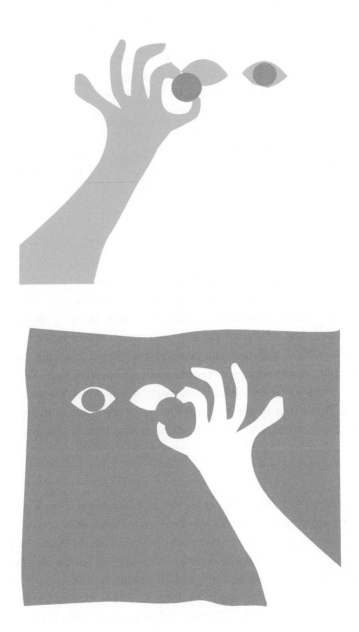

That which we do not see makes up everything, everywhere

8

THAT WHICH IS UNSEEN

We live in the physical world most of the time. This is the realm we understand. In the physical world, there are things we can feel, hear, taste and see. Sometimes, whether by design, by accident or circumstance, we do also experience the non-physical realm; the spiritual realm of existence. We occasionally separate from the physical senses and live in another dimension, if only for a second. That is the dimension we do not see. It is a separate reality as Carlos Castaneda would express it. The ancient philosophers would say that it is everything you cannot see that makes up all that you do see. In point of fact, you cannot see atoms, but they make up everything that is physical and everything we see. Further, they are moving in solid "inanimate" objects, although you cannot see that they are alive.

These occasional other dimensional experiences are rare in most people's lives. In fact, it is probable that many people are bound to the physical realm throughout their entire existence, without ever once knowing the power of other realities. And who is to say definitively how many other realities and dimensions there may be, even now, at this moment in time. As we grow in spirit and knowledge, we become aware of so much more than the standard convention of life we have been taught and to which we have been conditioned. That is not to detract from the order, discipline and structure that such training provides to our civilization. It has, after all taken us from "pith-ecus" to "sapiens." But those advances are of the Body and Brain, not necessarily of the Mind and Spirit.

Let us now discuss the discipline where the physical realm is no longer in control. This is a discipline where the Mind is in a conscious, then unconscious state whereby it creates a Balance between the Brain and the Body. Eastern spiritual traditions provide many examples of this type of " Mind over Body." For instance, Tibetan priests can lower their breathing and heart rates to almost imperceptible levels through mindfulness and meditation. They are in the Body, but through a process of physical abandonment, they reach a new level of peace, balance and enlightenment. It begins with the Mind.
Meditation is one way to experience the unseen and also a way to release your body from the physical realm. There are many forms of meditation and there is no one method that works best for everyone. As you may know, meditation is an ancient art and science. Yet it may be new for you. As Arthur Ash, the

great tennis icon stated for those bound by fear and inaction:

Start where you are
Use what you have
Do what you can

My approach is simple.

As you improve your results you can advance to different elements in the meditation including more difficult physical postures etc. In time, you will also develop your own unique method of arriving at mindfulness. These are the Nebula Stages you will experience using my method. This is the Nebula Exchange.

Nebula Step One:
Dedicate yourself to a few moments of reflection. Stop all outside activities. Be physically at rest. Have no interruptions. For now, position your body in a place of comfort, whether on the floor, a couch, chair or even in bed. The idea here is that your body's comfort should not be an issue to deal with at this time. You are going to abandon your body soon and it will happen more quickly and peacefully if it is comfortable.

Nebula Step Two:
Be aware of your breathing. Slowly clear your mind of the day's activities and thoughts. Reconcile all unresolved issues and release your connection to them. See and feel them drift away from you in your mind's eye. Unresolved issues disappear into the mist. They are no longer a part of you as you proceed to a clear Mind. Be aware of your breathing.

Nebula Step Three:
As you inhale, feel the energy come in through the top of your head and pass through your body. As you slowly exhale, feel the energy flow through and out of your body through your feet, cleansing you at each breath and powering your Mind at each breath.

Nebula Step Four:
Be aware of your breath. Freeze time into the "Now." There is no Past or Future. Now is the only Eternity and you are in it. There is no Time. There are no chains to hold you in time. Time is an illusion. If it can be measured, it is a prison. Choose to not be imprisoned by Time by any measure. The "Now" is constant and present. It is the only place in which you can reside and

exist. This is your choice. In a very real sense, it is only Now that is Eternal. Breathe....

Nebula Step Five
Breathe. Now leave your Body. You can no longer feel your Body. It is lighter and transparent. You are nowhere and everywhere in the Eterniverse. You are energy and thought. The power of the Eterniverse is yours. Breathe. Enjoy the abandonment and Surrender. Peace and strength wash over you. Breathe... Your heart beats slowly.
This is both peaceful and overwhelming.
Do this as long as you wish to be in this place.
It is here that you can control pain and emotions.

Nebula Step Six:
Start to feel your Body again as you come out of your mindful journey. Without touching your Body, feel your scalp, arms, legs, fingers, face, eyes and lips. Your Body is also healing itself. It is your temporary vessel.

Nebula Step Seven:
Breathe. Open your eyes. Wind down slowly. Breathe but not deeply.
Be mindful of the stunning physical beauty of this world as well as the Nebula you just experienced. Be mindful that the probability of you existing and being here is incalculable. It is a miracle....
Feel your Balance and Power.

Nebula Step Eight:
Share your strength with others. Love and Knowledge multiply when shared. They do not divide.
It is not likely that you will remember all these steps the first time you engage in these meditations. Start by practicing the first two, then three and four, until you are just flowing through all eight Steps.

It takes practice. I have been practicing and enjoying this for over 20 years and I can still improve the experience and results. With much practice, I have developed this experience to the point that I can make this happen during a business meeting or while driving. These experiences are very real. They are not a contrivance. They are strong and Powerful.

Again, as you practice these steps, you will find that some approaches and techniques will work better for you than others. You will also find that you will develop your very own style. Just feel free and let go. One step forward and the path will reveal itself to you.

Once when I vacationed in Mexico, I spent too much time in the sun, shirtless. I experienced severe sunburn because I loathe sunscreen. Upon my return home, my upper torso was starting to burn and itch terribly. It got progressively worse. It started to itch in the most painful way I have ever experienced. It became unbearable to the point I felt like a thousand ants were biting me. I felt helpless. The Mind was overcome by the Brain. Then I thought, "It's time to practice what you preach." I started my exercise and slowly went through the process of abandoning my Body. Slowly, the thousand points of pain reduced to 950, then 750, then 500. I could sense the pain leaving my Body until it was completely gone. It took about 15 minutes, but it worked. It was something you couldn't see, but it existed, nonetheless. The Mind conquered the Brain.

Another time I went to the doctor for a physical exam. He was performing all the normal tests when he told me to relax because he was going take my blood pressure and check my heart rate. I took him seriously, so I instantly went into a quick abandon Body mode and my Body reacted. He did the test. He asked me "Are you a long-distance runner or something?" I asked why. He said, "your heartbeat is very slow, almost dangerously slow!" I responded, "Well, you told me to relax, so I did." He replied, " You couldn't possibly have done that." I said, "I just did." "Well let's do it again but just be normal," he said. We did, and he was happy with the higher pulse rate.

In this physical realm, it is easy to forget how very powerful the realm of the invisible really is. Everything we cannot see, makes up everything we do see. Part of that realm is the Mind and Spirit. Things we do not see, yet they are so very powerful. Be aware and mindful of the presence of those things you do not see, but that make up the entirety of the Eterniverse.

Giving and Recieving

Each hand washes the other

9.

GIVING AND RECIEVING

At first glance, we would think that Giving and Receiving are at opposite ends of the spectrum. As you think about both of these acts, they are so closely intertwined that they are virtually indiscernible. It is almost the same comparison we made earlier about "who has what?" Do you have things, or do things have you?

It is a wonderful experience to Give. It is rewarding, fulfilling and dutiful. It fills your heart and soul with a joyful feeling. If you know how to Receive, that too is a transcendent experience.

When you think of the great religious and spiritual traditions of the world, you cannot help but be reminded that they emphasize the act of giving and sharing. There is an old saying;

Give without remembering,
Take without forgetting.

I have always tried, albeit not always successfully, to remember that short but powerful message.

Human nature being what it is, it seems that when we give, we want not only ourselves, but others including the recipient, to always remember that we gave something. It is as if we must keep an accounting of it. Think of all the things that can be given, both physical objects and spiritual blessings. It also seems that some people who give, want the whole world to know about it. They make a big production out of the entire act. As the Bible says, "They have received their reward." The entire philosophy of giving and receiving graciously is the goal, however our egos, our pride, our embarrassment and even our envy get the better of us and obscure a beautiful act or acts that should instead be liberating.

Think for a moment that your friend needs help paying his rent or mortgage payment. He needs $1000.00. He's embarrassed by his situation and you know him well enough to know that he's a hard worker, honorable and wouldn't ask unless he really needed the money. Somehow, for some reason, he's in a predicament, perhaps not of his own making. What's more, you have the money and you can either loan it or give it to him. What would you do? Would you launch an inquisition and try to illicit every last detail of his situation, not because you need the information, but because you have the advantage. Would you then go into lecture mode and "teach" him what he should be doing and where he erred so he wouldn't be in this situation? Then you loan or give him the money and follow it up with a discourse as to how generous you are and how lucky he is to have you as a friend. Next you tell the whole world what you did and how much you helped your friend. All of this is self-aggrandizement.

It's somewhat of an exaggeration of course, but while we might not put a voice to those thoughts, they would pass through our minds. We feel so good about giving that we can't help ourselves. It's natural. Later we discuss Forgiveness and Reconciliation. Both of these are acts of Giving, and when we experience this kind of Giving that has nothing to do with the physical, it is euphoric!!! The feeling we get after Giving, is a natural and spiritual high.
I think it is impossible to separate the act of sincere giving from the euphoria that follows. All of which brings me to the point of this discussion.

Is there really a difference between Giving and Receiving? We have been taught that Giving selflessly and with Purity of Intent is virtue. But when we give, we always Receive something in return. Perhaps we Receive more than we have given. We don't think about it that way because we honestly want to give sincerely with no expectation of recompense. We are not asking for a reward, (such as a credit towards salvation), at least not overtly. Giving can even be a private, quiet act that no one can see, as opposed to an ostentatious public act that is shown and promoted on TV and the press. The reality is that when we give, we are expecting and even relying on that phenomenal feeling of satisfaction we *Receive*, after we have Given. Perhaps we are hard wired this way so that we act in a God like manner. We Give because we Receive satisfaction and a feeling of well-being in return. In many ways the person who is Giving, is Receiving more than the person who is the recipient. What does all of this have to do with Balance and Power?

It is the understanding at a deeper level of who we are and why we do things. It is a study about what moves us and motivates us. It is about understanding and knowing ourselves. It is also important to understand that when we Give, there is some underlying, subliminal and self-serving motive. That is not a bad thing. It is simply important to know and understand this dynamic and that there is something else happening.

We gain Balance and Power by living our lives in a greater understanding of our actions and motivations. It is through this knowledge and understanding that we can grow and develop a deep and pure sense of selflessness; that we can Give without conditions, with Purity of Intent.

Be Undefeatable

*"He said he could never scale that wall,
and the truth is, he was the only one guarding it."*

10

BE UNDEFEATABLE

The Defeatist	The Undefeatable
Mental prisons	Possibility thinking
It will never work	Let's get started
I can't do it	I believe in myself
I'm afraid	Fear knocked at the door...Courage answered
I'm a failure	Failure is part of Success
I'm not good enough	God gave me immeasurable gifts
I can't win	I am Undefeatable!!!

Mental conditioning is a powerful thing. It is powerful both from a positive and negative perspective. It has been said that if you believe you will succeed or if you believe you will fail...you are right. As with the prior discussion we have had about the knowledge of good and evil, I think about how the attitudes for success or failure arise and manifest themselves in a person. Are those attitudes innate or are they learned?

When I was in prison, inmates would always ask me what I was going to do when I got into the "world". My response was always the same; "I am going to make money and I am going to succeed." "How do you know that?", they would ask. Again, my response was always the same; "Because making money and being successful is a habit."

I believe Success is a habit; unfortunately, so is failure. I believe the Brain and Mind can be conditioned for Success. But this discussion is not solely about Success and how we can experience Success in its many forms. So called Success can be viewed as excelling in financial, educational, career and other realms. I had always felt I had a good understanding and appreciation as to what was real and valuable in life, however my time in prison refined my views regarding what is of real substance in life. Yes, I knew I would make money and be successful, however, the real treasure I discovered was in adversity. Adversity provides a platform from which many strong and lasting characteristics and positive habits can be developed. For many, Adversity is defeat.
Adversity is a coin with two sides

There is so very much more than being successful in the conventional paradigm.

I recall getting ready to walk through the gates at the prison to drive to El Paso, Texas, where I would board a bus, unsupervised and on my own for the first time in two years. I was to report to the half-way house in Albuquerque, New Mexico. As I walked through the gate, other than the $200.00 I had on my prison debit card, I had no money, no car or home to go to. My girlfriend had left me. I had no job or income. All of my businesses were closed down. I was estranged from my two sons.

For the first time in my adult life, I had nothing.
Yet for the first time in my life, I had everything!

I had everything in front of me. I had every opportunity to pursue. I had a clean slate upon which to build. I had Peace. I had Power. I had Purpose. While it was somewhat unnerving, I almost couldn't contain my enthusiasm. What an amazing and unequalled opportunity I had! It was as if God was telling me..." Ok, you think you are such a bad ass? Let's see what you've got." I could now start from the ground up and rebuild my life in the world. It was time to find a way. It was time to follow my own advice about purpose, toughness, character, focus, patience, forgiveness and empathy. It was time to place one foot forward and let the path reveal itself to me. I am fortunate that I never had the "poor me" attitude. There was always a path to move forward.

I remember as a young man, my father asked me to move a large boulder, probably fully aware that I couldn't move it with purely physical effort, unaided by tools or devices. I gallantly tried my very best, not wanting to disappoint him. I tried valiantly but with no success. I told him in Spanish, "I can't." He looked at me in a stern and piercing way and said without hesitation, "*No hay tal cosa, que no se puede.*" ("There is no such thing as 'it can't be done.")
He then proceeded to place a smaller stone close to the boulder; and using a 4"x 4" piece of wood, and the smaller stone as a fulcrum, he easily moved the boulder. Although, I kind of felt like he cheated, I realized the value of the lesson. Find a way to do it. Figure it out. Think. Move. Try something. Just get started. Don't be defeated by the challenge. The lesson is simple but powerful. I never forgot it. Seek solutions, not obstacles.

Our lives are replete with events and challenges that allow us the opportunity to employ a mindset, an attitude, that says "I can do this!!!", "I will not be defeated by this." The alternative is an attitude of defeatism. It can appear to be an easier way, but it only appears that way. Remember we said that success and failure are habits? Being Undefeatable is also a habit. And how do you acquire a habit? Practice and repetition. Being Undefeatable is no different. We do have a choice between Surrender and Success. It is a mindset; it is a conditioning of the Mind to not be defeated by the things in this world that make people Surrender. That is not to say that it is always easy. It isn't. We are confronted with so many different challenges in this frenzied world that it is a wonder we don't all go crazy and Surrender. But Surrender, we mustn't.

Virtually everything can challenge us with elements for potential defeat or Surrender;

marriage
children
parents
employment
unemployment
self-employment
employees
bosses
debt
income
school
bullying
your weight
exercise
health
drugs and alcohol
smoking
friendships
unrequited love
sports
unrealized goals

Sometimes, life is very difficult. That's a lot of weight and worry we burden ourselves with. Depending on how critical any of these are to you in your life, they can take you to the brink of Surrender. As you think back on these challenges, you know that you have been there. Close to breaking or actually breaking down.

I have found that one of the keys to meeting these challenges is the art of Inquiry and Listening as we have discussed before. Sometimes the Inquiry and Listening is with yourself. Sometimes it involves others. What does this mean to you? What is Inquiry and Listening when confronted with these challenges?

Take any one of the challenges shown above. The biggest challenge with any of these or any others that come your way, is **understanding** it. First you must understand the challenge, and to do that you must face it without prejudice, pre-conceptions, Perspective and Justification. That is a lot to ask, but that is what is required if you are come to terms with the challenge.

Being Undefeatable doesn't mean winning in the conventional sense of winning. Being Undefeatable means that your Mind and Spirit are not broken. While I was in prison, I was under the total control of the government. What I ate, where I slept, what work I did, the clothes I wore, what time I arose and went to bed, the length of my phone calls, my salary (five cents an hour); everything was out of my control and everything about me and my life was in prison; incarcerated....

except my Mind and Spirit

I couldn't have Peace about any of those things in prison unless I understood them. It is important to mention here that understanding something doesn't mean you like it. It means you go through a process of internal Inquiry and Listening to grasp **what** is occurring and **why** it is happening. If it is to be done with Purity of Intent, it requires deep and personal introspection. If the person you love suddenly decides to leave you, you will likely be devastated, and that devastation will likely adversely affect your mental, physical, spiritual and even financial health. You can't understand what happened and why it happened, yet it did happen. The process of understanding this and not being defeated by it is simple, but difficult. The first thing most people do is blame themselves when something like that happens. But the first thing to do is simply to acknowledge that the event occurred. It doesn't help to be in a state of mind that says, "I can't believe he did that!"

It happened. Things happen. It is what it is. Whether "*it*" is that I was confined in a prison cell or whether *it* is that your significant other left you. You are, where you are. Yes, you are hurting and afraid, and you could be heading for a dark time. But how can you unfreeze and move forward? How can you gain from this? How can you harvest good from this trial and tribulation? Understand the situation and make a plan.

I understood that being in prison would be difficult if I allowed it to be difficult. Because I knew it was inevitable, I decided that I would make myself immune to the feelings of despair, loneliness, abandonment, self-pity, regret, blame, self-doubt, suspicion, loss of control and generally all negative thoughts. I understood that I could gain power from the Adversity, or I could allow those challenges to weaken and defeat me. I understood that it was going to be difficult. I made a commitment to myself that I would not abandon myself, because that is all I had left.

I also knew that I was now in a place where I could grow physically, spiritually, emotionally and mentally, if I allowed the prison experience to teach me and temper me. I knew that if I harvested the opportunity (and yes, I did consider it an opportunity), I would grow in ways that only Adversity can teach you. I knew that if my Mind was right, I would gain Peace, Purpose and Power. In fact, that is exactly what happened. The experience was transformed from punishment to Power.

You should read that paragraph again.

That was my Perspective. If you can change your Perspective from fear and hurt, to one of opportunity and Power, you too will transcend the challenges.

You've seen it many times, in countless people and circumstances. There are those who Surrender and those who are Undefeatable. You may have wondered how people become Undefeatable. What are their triggers? What are their motivations? From where does this indomitable, undefeatable attitude come? How can they be so strong and so unaffected by dire and crushing circumstances and events? How can they just keep going? How can I be like that? *Can* I be like that?

The answer is, unconditionally, *yes*! The reality is that in this life and in this society, while some challenges seem insurmountable, our challenges are relatively pale by comparison to other cultures and humans throughout history. What seems life shattering to you in your *vida loca* world, would be laughable to others in history and to many others living a crushing life today, many of whom would love to walk in your shoes. This is not meant to trivialize issues in your life, but simply to place things in Perspective and Balance.

When I think of the events in my life that could have been cause for Surrender, I think of Nelson Mandela and his decades of illegal imprisonment; Anne Frank, her persecution and death; George Washington at Valley Forge; Mother Teresa living in abject poverty and disease and millions of black slaves in the New World whose lives and families were stolen for the enrichment of others.

These are but a handful from which we can take guidance and lessons. They are examples that you recognize. There are millions more who have lived their lives as Undefeatables with no one being aware of it and no-one knowing who they were. There are some among you now, fighting the good fight and refusing to Surrender. They and you are Undefeatables too. Some of them are Undefeatable as public figures. Most however, fight their good fight in silence, character and integrity, no one knowing their challenge. That too is Godliness. They have found their Enthéos; God within. That Undefeatable may be you.

But the question remains. How did they become Undefeatable? Why do they not Surrender? I believe that all of us have the power to be Undefeatable. You have probably experienced this Power in some form at some time in your life, if only for a fleeting moment of Enlightenment. But how can we become Undefeatable as a way of life?"

I want to clarify that being Undefeatable is not an oppressive, winning at any cost, adversarial, "me too" or "me only" experience. It is not an arrogant position that announces to the world " I am right, no matter what" or " I will win and cannot be beat." On the contrary, it is a silent, positive, respectful and internal strength that you must recognize is in you.

Think of Mahatma Ghandi and his quiet, strong, peaceful, yet persevering actions and purpose. There was no arrogance there. Yet, he was Undefeatable. Nothing could defeat him, not even his physical death. Dr. Martin Luther King Jr. also serves as an example of Balance and Power and being a unique combination of force through peace.

The answer lies in you. Right now, at this very moment, you have the Power to be an Undefeatable. There is a physical, mental and spiritual reality to all of this. This is very real. However, the process doesn't work if you are not first aware of the Power that resides in you. It is as if there is an impenetrable shield protecting and surrounding you. Also be cognizant that the negative event, situation or person is seeking to steal your Strength and Power. Refuse to feed that negative fire. Do not Surrender.

Psalm 27

The Lord is my light and salvation
Of whom should I be afraid;
The Lord is my life's refuge,
Whom should I fear?
When evildoers come before me
to devour my flesh
My foes and my enemies
Themselves stumble and fall before me;
Through an army encamp against me,
My heart will not fear;
Through war be waged upon me,
Even then will I trust...
For he will hide me in his abode
In the day of trouble...
Give me not up to the wishes of my foes;
For false witnesses have risen up against me.
And such as breathe out violence...
Be stout hearted..........

Be Undefeatable.

Redemption

It fell from the heavens

11

REDEMPTION

I believe in Redemption...
> I believe in Forgiveness...
>> I believe in Rehabilitation...
>>> I believe in Reconciliation...

I believe in People's Goodwill.

Having been an inmate in a Federal government prison, I have experienced firsthand the entire process of arraignment, indictment, prosecution, sentencing, serving time in prison, serving time in a halfway house, home confinement and five years of probation. For a twenty-seven-month sentence in prison, in actuality, including pre-trial probation and post prison probation, amounted to an entire amount of time consumed of almost nine years. When my friends ask me what it was like, I say that it was like being devoured by the mouth of the dragon and being crapped out the back end. But sadly, it does not end there. Convicted felons carry that cross and scarlet letter for the rest of their lives even if they have successfully served their time and re-integrated into society, which by the way is no simple task. That is one significant reason for such high rates of recidivism. The American system of justice is not forgiving even after the time has been served. Human judgment only exacerbates the situation.

Yes, there are forgiving and accepting people who support ex-cons, however, the overall public perception and resulting judgment is that such people will always be criminals, will never be rehabilitated and are a constant danger to society. They are not to be trusted. In fact, in this country, even a person charged with a crime who is ultimately acquitted, is suspect for the rest of their life. You hear the whispers..." isn't that the guy who was charged with embezzlement?" or didn't he get accused of child molestation?" Even though the person was not guilty, the judgment persists. The hypocrisy runs very deep. But there is hypocrisy in the prisons as well. In talking to most fellow inmates, I was somewhat taken by surprise that almost all of them claimed that they were innocent, were entrapped unfairly, that the government just had it out for them or many other excuses that supposedly exculpated them. I think I was one of the few who admitted that I committed a crime. The thing that bothered me the most however, was that they felt that my biggest crime was not that I had committed a crime, but that I got caught!!

I still struggle with that one.

I wrote a few personal thoughts in my first book entitled "Enthéos, God Within", some of which discuss my experiences in prison. For me, prison was a cathartic experience. It was a necessary part of my life. Prison was an experience without which my life would be incomplete. Yes, it was difficult in every possible way, but the harshness, the challenges, the loss of personal identity, the solitude and isolation, the sense of helplessness, the unpredictability (and the bad food), prepared me for a banquet beyond comprehension. One I would never have realized was a banquet at all unless, and until, I didn't have it. It is now a part of my path that I embrace. I hope I touched people's lives in prison just as I work to mentor people of all ages and careers today in the world. It is difficult to explain and in some ways very hard to believe, but somehow, for some reason that is not yet fully understood, I had Peace the moment I stepped into that 100 degree transport van filled with 15 other inmates, and all through the two years I was incarcerated. Strangely, I found more Peace as time progressed, so much so that I didn't keep track of time. Here is a poem I wrote while in prison. It talks of experiencing freedom while in prison.

I Fagio

"the Hearing in the Heart is for those Enlightened"

(I Fly)

My awakening today is *Luminescent and the Energy is thick like fog;

the vision into their Collective Soul is uplifted by their Celestial Harmony.

The anticipation overwhelms me. I have witnessed their Heavenly Dance before,

but today, now, this morning is more Intimate.
For on this day, in this time, at this place, I think I know what I shall see.

10,000 Sentinels Standing Strong against the wind;

No! Not wind! The Breath of Elohim under wing.

The Keys to Balance and Power

10,000 golden breasts bursting forth against the Sun from arboreal perches. And in each, beats their song in soulful unison.

The Symphony is frenzy to a shallow spirit,

but the Hearing in the Heart is for those Enlightened.

10,000 voices singing praises to on High to a crescendo;

one song, a Reverent Rejoicing.

But what is their Purpose; Their meaning here?

They live free within these prison walls, immune to rules and cells and keys.

What shall we learn from their Unchained Nobility?

The answer now takes flight.

Then these 10,000 Strands of Life singing now with one Pure Voice

bring my contemplation back to the now.

Their Sacred Utterance rises to Primeval Shout

in **Sacrosanct Exuberance....

Then.... in One Mind and Soul together,

SILENCE....

Now 10,000 golden jewels take flight at once.

One strong breath lifts them all together.

Incomprehensible is a word unworthy

in description of their Eloquence.

These Ten Thousand are but

One Mind, One Body, One Spirit,

their aerial ballet, Honey Flowing from Heaven

like the Word and Reason of Shaddai,

The Almighty,

sweet to eyes so starved for Beauty.

And now upon being witness to this Sacred Orchestra,

I come to know why they traveled here;

To free my own imprisoned Mind and Soul.

I shed the Chains of Servitude and lift myself with them;

Now, Ten Thousand and One....

I FAGIO!! I FAGIO!!

I FLY!! I FLY!!

*Luminescent: Radiant; shining bright with light from within

**Sacrosanct: Sacred; respected; hallowed

What a wonderful journey most of us make in this world. Unfortunately, the joy and exhilaration of it is seldom fully recognized or appreciated. Most of us understand Redemption as a religious or spiritual experience which will occur upon our physical transformation at death, into what I call Enlightenment; *the knowledge and awareness of everything.* So much has been written about Redemption. "We are redeemed" from this or that fate. We are redeemed from the eternal fires of hell! It is almost as if helpless and weak, unknowing and unsuspecting beings are being rescued like some hopeless character in a Greek or Shakespearean play, by the "Deus Ex Machina" swooping down from the heavens (which was actually physical infrastructure of the theatre), to save the otherwise lost creature. How innovative. The "Deus Ex (est) Machina" theatrical device comes from Latin meaning "God is (in) a

Machine", or "God, the Machine." This was Divine Intervention theater style in the Shakespearean era.

The common thought is that the person could not be redeemed were it not for a redeemer. Is it possible to experience Redemption from within? Many belief systems in the world have created a redeemer type of personage and deity. I believe that such a redeemer personage was necessary for people to have hope for a greater existence after this physical life. The belief is that to have eternal life one must be redeemed. That is not to say that the God Entity or the Universal Consciousness is not a Redeemer. It is to say that perhaps we really don't know or have a full understanding of what that is. Nonetheless, I believe I have experienced Redemption through God Within.

"True freedom is of the Mind and Soul

No shackle can bind you and keys will not set you free."

From Entheos, God Within

It's strange that sometimes the hopeless character or the lost person does not know that it needs rescuing or that it is even possible or desired to be redeemed. The Redemption to which this chapter is dedicated is much more an event of liberation and freedom that has at its core, a spiritual strength and awakening and is fully lived by the person who experiences Redemption. I have shared with you some thoughts about prison life and how it can change a person. If you read the poem above, "I Fagio" (I Fly), you can understand the most exhilarating feeling of Redemption as I felt it. I was honored that my fellow inmates asked me to write about this phenomenon, and so I did.

Let's talk about other forms of liberation and imprisonment. How often have you experienced the imprisonment of a job, a career, running a business, the endless and unforgiving hustle of trying to achieve more, to get more things? This is how it was for me before I was indicted. I was that person reaching for more accomplishments, recognition, money and all things of this world. Because there is always the threat of losing these things, you can feel like you are living in darkness, under a cloud of negativity, where something, anything, is about to go wrong. Impending doom, mental and spiritual lethargy. Nothing seems Right. It is precisely at times like this that one can Surrender. You can continue along that path, or not. And while it may seem to those not so afflicted that you should just "suck it up", the reality is that these may be the most challenging of all our experiences. For those of you who have never felt the deep despair of depression, know that its real and life altering, and in some cases, life ending. A friend of mine calls suicide a permanent solution to a temporary problem.

My brother was addicted to drugs. His name is Gaspar; it is one of the names of the three wise men of the Bible. One of the Zoroastrian priests. He used heroin for many years. He was exceedingly talented. He was an artist who worked in wood, paint on stone, carvings, and he built stunning fireplaces. He was also a builder in the now almost lost art of constructing homes with adobe bricks made with one's own hands. He was a powerful man and a powerful presence. He was at once kind and when provoked, vicious. I remember once we were standing in the street at my parent's home. It was a somewhat rural place close to the Rio Grande. There were stray dogs up and down the river bosque and we never had a concept of buying a dog or buying dog food or the idea of a veterinarian. They just showed up one day, stayed for a few years then just disappeared, but we embraced them as if they were family while they stayed.

One day a small dog was making his way down the street and a car suddenly ran over him. The dog shrieked and rolled away to the side of the road and appeared to be in excruciating pain, and possibly close to death. I had seen this before and it looked bad. My brother calmly and confidently walked over to the suffering creature, placed his foot very softly and gently on the dog's body, crouched down over him and placed his hand on him. Immediately, the dog stopped moving and stopped crying. I thought he was now dead. My brother looked into him with the most peaceful look I think I've ever seen and talked to him in a very low voice. I couldn't distinguish what he spoke. Suddenly, the dog sprang to life, stood up and walked away. It was one of the most powerful events I have ever witnessed.

Much later when he started using drugs, I saw that strength and kindness in him, in his face, but he knew he was trapped in the darkness. It was devastating to witness the metamorphosis in this child of God, my brother and my friend.

He died of an overdose of heroin, perhaps self-inflicted and no less fatal than a bullet. I miss him and often wonder if he finally felt Redemption. And I feel that his physical death must have liberated him into Enlightenment.

"Do not go gentle into that good night,
Old age should burn and rave at close of day;
Rage, rage against the dying of the light...

Grave men, near death, who see with blinding sight...
Rage, rage against the dying of the light."
-Dylan Thomas

As living, feeling and conscious human beings, of this time and place and in this existence as part of this Eterniverse, we would like to experience Redemption in this world. We should participate in this Redemption not only of ourselves, but of others. God has given you special gifts. Most people travel through this life without recognizing their unique gifts. Learn to have a "listening" for these gifts. I submit to you that if you share with people, you will discover your gifts. I am not referring to physical gifts such as possessions or beauty. This has to do with the intangibles you have that are the most meaningful. The most valuable gifts you have are the things that are not physical things. They are things that cannot be seen. Listening is a gift you can share with someone that can liberate them, and in exchange, you gain Balance and Power. Start with listening and go from there. You will be surprised by what transpires.

Visiting a stranger in prison or in the hospital can redeem a person's spirit. Sharing time with a lonely elderly person in a nursing home can give the gift of hope and caring. Cooking a meal for a friend shares a personal part of you with them. Each of these is a redemptive act. It is in doing for others that in a very real way, we are Redeeming ourselves. It liberates our spirits and frees us from darkness. It gives us Balance in our lives. It's not about me, it's about us. As if we are all part of one eternal and universal consciousness, each of us dependent on the other and on each other's unique gifts. And in such manner, we take what would be lost and discarded and make it into a harmonic masterpiece.

THE TOUCH OF THE MASTER'S HAND

Twas battered and scarred
and the auctioneer thought it scarcely worth his while
to waste much time on the old violin,
But held it up with a smile;
"What am I bidden good folks," he cried,
"who will start the bidding for me?"
"A dollar."
"a dollar; then two!"
"Only two? Two dollars;
and who'll make it three?"
"Three dollars once; Three dollars twice;
Going for three..."

But no, from the room, far back, a gray-haired man
came forward and picked up the bow;
Then wiping the dust from the old violin,
and tightening the loose strings,
He played a melody pure and sweet
as caroling angels sing.

The music ceased and the auctioneer,
with a voice that was quiet and low, said;
"What am I bid for the old violin?"
And he held it up with the bow.
"A thousand dollars, and who'll make it two?"
"Two thousand";
"And who'll make it three?"
"Three thousand once, three thousand twice,
and going and gone," said he.
The People cheered, but some of them cried.
"We do not understand what changed its worth."
Swift came the reply:

"The touch of the Master's hand."

And many a man with life out of tune,
and battered and scarred with sin,
is actioned cheap to the thoughtless crowd,

much like the old violin.
A mess of pottage, a glass of wine;
a game, and he travels on.
He is going once and going twice.
He's going and almost gone.

But the Master comes,
and the foolish crowd never can quite understand
The worth of a soul
And change that's wrought
By the touch of the Master's hand.

Myra "Brooks" Welch.

Surrender

There are two kinds

12

SURRENDER

*"It is reasonable to say (that) Surrender is just an idea
that keeps people from leading (their) lives".* – Rumi

In your Book of Life, notwithstanding the omni-present philosophical arguments regarding free will (choice) versus causal determinism (all things are pre-determined), you make choices or perhaps you only think you make choices throughout your life that contribute to the molding and creation of your individual and highly unique life's path. Each of these choices adds a level of improbability to the knowledge and actuality of your future just as did all of the choices that were made by those who preceded you. The decisions we make are both conscious and unconscious, and made with a conscience or lack of conscience; deliberate and not deliberate. Sometimes we make a decision or choose a path by doing nothing. A choice to do nothing is a choice, nonetheless. Sometimes we fool ourselves into thinking and believing that when we choose to do nothing we aren't really acting and therefore not responsible. We are indeed acting by choosing not to act. The conscious failure to act is a decision you can make and such a failure to act can change the course of events every bit as much as deciding to act. It is interesting that legal documents have a phrase in them that state that someone can be culpable "for any acts or failure to act".

Think for a moment about the countless decisions you make daily. You might say that in your job and in your life, things are so routine and established that there is little to no decision making involved. Think about your daily life routine. Think about how it starts and how it progresses throughout the day and how it ends at home. Whether you do or not do certain things are things you decide to do or not to do, nonetheless. Obviously, there are different levels of decisions that one makes during the day. Some are very minor and seemingly insignificant like the soap or shampoo you will use this morning or if you will have your eggs fried or scrambled or even hard boiled. Others are somewhat important that can affect certain things in your life such as your lunch plans or which projects you will focus on today. Still others may be life and career altering such as deciding to be a whistle-blower. If you work in a job that you can't tolerate anymore but you keep working at that job, you are making a decision to stay, because you are doing nothing to change that status. You are silent on the issue. You are making a decision to remain in that employment prison which is one of many prisons into which we self-incarcerate. Well, you might say that you can't afford to leave your current employment because of the fear of losing the benefits, the pay, retirement and the security. In that case, it is fear that drives your decision. That may be true and valid, but you are still making a decision. If you have dreamed of having your own business and being independent, you would likely have to sacrifice those things to pursue your dream. But it isn't an easy thing to do, so you make the decision to stay in the current job and situation. You make a decision to remain at your employment prison instead of pursuing your dream. I am not saying that it is a bad thing to be committed to a job even if you are not thrilled with it, or that you are doing something wrong or that you should feel guilt. Quite the contrary, all I am saying is that it is important in your daily Reconciliation to know what the Truth is in your unique life, to know what you are deciding, why you are making that decision and to acknowledge that you are the one who is making the decisions.

Believe it or not, going through a thought process about it can give you Peace about your decision. Ignoring it as something you will maybe think about someday only muddles your clarity because the issue is not Reconciled within yourself; it is not settled. Another benefit of thorough Reconciliation about life issues can provide you with the reasons and rationale to pursue your dream. This process can apply to virtually any situation where you must make a decision. How does this relate to Surrender? It relates to Surrender because you are facing the issue head on even if you are fearful of the mental discussion and the resulting answer, Truth or decision. But at least the decision will be purposeful and conscious. Have the mental discussion by simply taking the time to have the mental discussion. It can be a fearful thing at first, however if you practice this exercise you can Reconcile the "who and the what of you" and have Peace. Albert Einstein developed many of his complex theories by having "thought experiments" which helped him develop ideas and solutions to problems. He simply thought about issues and developed potential solutions. We now know that his General and Special theories of relativity came about during his many thought experiments and he changed the scientific world. You can do the same. You can approach the issue with purpose and regardless of the decision at least it is your work and is not left in the nebulous world of indecision or some third party telling you what is wrong with you or with your life. This gives you Power because you approached and faced the issue, even if in fear, and decided. I didn't Surrender to "maybe", "I wonder" or "what if", which would lead to "Could have" "Should have" and "Would have".

For all sad words of tongue and pen, the saddest are these,
'It might have been.'

Stop for a moment and consider some thing, some issue that you have not Reconciled in your life, whether it is a weight problem, chronic tardiness, gossiping, financial issues, too much social media or making up with someone for whom you care. Now without any interruptions, think about that issue for a full ten minutes. Ask yourself these questions and commit your thoughts to writing.

How did this start?
What was the catalyst that gave this issue life? What caused it?
How do I feel about it? (be Truthful, but don't be too hard on yourself)
What would I like to do about it? What result and resolution do I need or want?
Do I really want to do this?
How can I do this? Write a plan for how you can make it work.
Can I make a commitment to myself and to the Eterniverse to do it?
Do I still *really* want to do this?
If you don't, can you accept the decision you are making?
When will I start to implement the plan?

Whether your decision is to do it or not to do it, at least you made a thoughtful and purposeful decision. You have the Power and the Balance.
Have a conversation with a friend or family member about this with whom you feel very comfortable. Make some time for both of you to do this analysis about some issue that each of you selects for this process. It will be an enjoyable experience and a Reconciliation in and of itself to go through the process. Do it together. It will be healing, revealing and cathartic. The other benefit is that you can support each other in the accomplishment of your respective choices.

It reminds me of Lent in a way. The Catholic observance of Lent sometimes gets a bad rap because it seems to the outside world that Catholics are doing something kind of silly when they "give up" something like drinking alcoholic beverages or sweets. The reality is that it has a far deeper meaning and goal. We are to consider our lives, our blessings, challenges, relationships, and our weaknesses and frailties. We consider something that we would like to improve in our lives to make us better and more spiritually evolved. The process we have discussed is very similar to the Lenten decision. Many Catholics don't give up anything. Instead, they consider what they would like to improve in their lives such as being more mindful of other people's feelings and the condition in their own lives. They think about it and consider whether or not they can make a commitment to the decision they are about to make. Then they decide and make a plan and implement it. The goal is to make this temporary Lenten act a permanent part of an improvement in our lives. Step by step, we can change and improve ourselves and make ourselves more Powerful and Balanced.

In many faith traditions, Surrender is a desirable thing. It is a thing to be achieved and strived for. In many ways, that kind of Surrender is the goal of the discussions in this book as well. That kind of Surrender is a worthwhile endeavor because it releases and liberates us from burdens that we carry that detract from, rather than enhance, our path. Most faiths from Hindu to Buddhist and from Christianity to Islam have a tradition of Surrender of oneself from the physical bonds of this life to achieve Enlightenment or Nirvana in some form while here on Earth. Buddhists celebrate a very special form of Surrender to what they call the "Universal Soul". These ancient beliefs and pursuits are inspiring. Seeking the Universal Soul means that there is some acknowledgment and understanding that there is such an existence and entity. We are constantly reminded, and we should never forget that many great and enlightened minds have passed through this Earth. We should not forget their messages. How uplifting it is to know that there are beings on Earth that dedicate their lives to this search.? How much more difficult is that search and that Surrender while we inhabit a planet and society that has so many physical plenitudes? It makes the effort that much more difficult, but the attainment that much more gratifying when achieved. It is our desire to achieve such Peace, Balance and Power in our brief lifetimes.

This next discussion is not about that kind of spiritual Surrender. It is about a different kind of Surrender. It is about how we "give up", how we throw in the towel; how we Surrender in a manner that subtracts from our lives instead of enhancing our lives.

Many of the choices we make or the thoughts we think involve the decision to continue on a positive path, a path of Enlightenment, Purity of Intent or simply choosing not to live in Darkness. On the other hand, we also make choices or give in to thoughts that lead to a dark Surrender. Sometimes we Surrender without knowing it. It happens often and is based in complacency and fear. It is very easy to become conditioned to virtually any activity or thought. Sometimes we are placed in a situation where we seemingly have no choices and the decisions are driven by nature such as the instinct to survive and live. We "decide" to fight for life. Some people decide to die. Sometimes due to neglect or because we ignore events, we have made a decision by default, to allow other forces and events to write that portion of our Book of Life. Some other force seems to take over. We have Surrendered that choice and yet by choosing to do nothing we are still making a choice. This is not to say that these decisions and choices or the lack of choosing are easy. Many times, they are not easy. But in many cases, we are choosing between doing the right thing even though it may be difficult and Surrendering to doing the wrong thing. And when we decide to continue, to live, to survive, to become Enlightened, to walk in the Light instead of Darkness and to win, all of the necessary forces align;

Strength	Commitment
Aggressiveness	Mental Acuity
Strategic	Thinking Endurance
Fear of Failure	Patience
Acceptance	Success

The decision you make to continue, to move forward is a victory, a success in and of itself, simply because it is not Surrender. Whether it is an event related to a relationship, education, learning, your career, health or an addiction, and provided any one of the above is not based on outside physical, mental or emotional abuse or oppression, the decision to continue is like deciding to live and breathe. Remember,
"every breath is a lifetime"

Conversely, one can decide to Surrender. Many times, this decision is more subtle and imperceptible, but it is a definite and identifiable event, nonetheless. The reason it is more subtle is because we don't want to admit a dark Surrender. We ignore that it is happening. For instance, when one is conscious of their weight and diet, at some imperceptible point in time, which we might not even be able to identify, a mini decision is made to surrender, or *not* to Surrender. You know what you should do to achieve your goals and desires, but you choose otherwise. The decision to Surrender in this case may be a minor event, but the subconscious mind gets accustomed to it and accepts each successive Surrender more easily and without objection, until it accepts it permanently. Then it becomes a habit.

People form habits and habits form futures.

It reminds me of the story of the frog that is placed in a frying pan in warm water. It is a nice warm comfortable place to be. Then the heat is turned up a little. Now it is nice and warm. It squirms a little when it gets hotter, then it gets used to it, accepts it, gets complacent and stops fighting. Then the temperature is raised just a little more, almost imperceptibly, and the frog squirms a little again, then once again gets used to it and stops fighting. He's relaxing. After all, he is adapting right? It sounds like a good thing and the right thing to do. Yet again and again the scenario is repeated as the heat is raised and the frog adjusts each time. Finally, after a while, the frog is cooked, and it didn't even know it was cooking. The process is insidious, and it occurs in our lives all of the time. We just get used to things and many times it is just convenient to ignore what is happening even though we may be very aware of it. We get accustomed to the heat and just ignore it and all the while we are cooking and Surrendering.

It is almost as if the Surrender emits a sigh of relief. It's over. No more trying. I give up.
One of the things we do in our lives is to make "e-greements". We make ego agreements with ourselves about how we will live our lives. We don't usually share these agreements with others because we don't want anyone to know our little secrets. Why? Because maybe they aren't totally honorable, and others wouldn't agree with them. They manifest themselves in many ways such as

private envy of another person's success,
private glee in the failure of someone we don't care for (shadenfreude)
secret snacks or drinks,
gossiping about another's misfortunes,
cursing out the slow-moving driver in front of us,
looking with disdain on a homeless person,
bragging about a good deed we have done
unfair judgment of another

Our human nature makes it easy to do these things even though we know we shouldn't do them, so we make e-greements with ourselves and do them anyway. This is a form of Surrender.

For instance, the decision to continue to learn or not learn, or to live in Light instead of Darkness, or not to do those things, is much the same. For a hundred different reasons one can choose to live in the positive or one can Surrender. Your Book of Life is full of these events and choices. You can stay in the game or let it drift away. And so it is with the events that shape this life of ours. The problem is that many times these small seemingly insignificant events and decisions are almost imperceptible, so we have to pay attention all the time and be conscious of what we are thinking and doing and how those things affect our paths, our lives and the lives of others.

Again, it is important to know that for most of us, these lessons and disciplines are not very easily learned. For many of us, it is a lifetime journey that will never end. We struggle daily to follow the positive path. But we must make the valiant effort to do better and to be better every day. Can we be better just today? Then we'll do it again tomorrow and the next day until it becomes a good habit. Fight the good fight; fight one more round. Do not go gentle into that goodnight. Don't ever give up. Don't Surrender.

Being conscious that we **can** choose, that we have the power to Surrender, or not Surrender, can help us to understand our lives better. We have such immense power within us that it is immeasurable. We have the Power of the Creator within us. Knowing and understanding and believing that we can harness that power can give us Balance and Power in our lives. We all want our lives to be orderly and laid out perfectly, but the reality is that many times our lives lack direction and are full of chaos. So, for this unplanned and frenzied life, let's provide some Balance to guide us along our path.

"IF you force your heart
And nerve and sinew
To serve your turn
Long after they are gone
And so, hold on
When there is nothing
In you except the will
Which says to them
HOLD ON! "

From the Poem "If" By Rudyard Kipling

You have goals and dreams. You want to accomplish certain things in your life's path. These are things that give your life Meaning and Purpose. Think for a minute about your own personalized bucket list. Many times, a bucket list is associated with the end of life here on Earth.

Isn't it interesting that so many of the things on such a bucket list don't include money or physical possessions? That is likely due to the realization that those possessions will not follow into the next existence. Suddenly, what is really important rises to the surface and reveals itself and the reason for its importance. Yes, it does take money to do a lot of the things on such a list, but if you could do those things without money, you would still do them. Hold on to those important things. Don't Surrender your heart, your mind and your soul. Don't give up. Follow these steps.

Start with small and achievable goals;
Set a timetable for each accomplishment;
Don't punish yourself if you don't succeed. Try again;
Stack one achievement alongside another;
You have something; It might be minor but start with that and build on it.
Each small success is one ingredient in the recipe for a great feast;
Stay focused and stay positive;
Don't Surrender to people who choose to live in Darkness;
If you are ill, help someone who is also ill;
If you are in depression, seek the company of positive people;
When you are depressed, help another who is depressed;
If you are broke, make one dollar, then another;
If you are dying, be thankful that you had a Book of Life like no other;
Live in Enlightenment, not in Darkness;
You are the master of your fate;
You are the captain of your soul;
Don't Surrender.

For God gave us a Spirit
Not of Fear
But of Power;
And Love
And Self Control.

Timothy 1:7

Nobody Likes a Caterwauler

Stand up.... take responsibility for yourself

13

NOBODY LIKES A CATERWAULER

Well, what exactly is a caterwauler? There is a dictionary version of the meaning, but to me, the word just shouts out "whiner", or "complainer"! And nobody likes a whiner or a complainer. Unfortunately, in our society today where people have so many rights instead of obligations and where "entitlement" is the word du jour, we can get to be caterwaulers pretty easily. Have you noticed that there is always something to complain about? Either the coffee is too hot or it's too cold. Or maybe the coffee is too weak and not as strong as you like it. We complain about virtually everything; from work to finances and everything in between. Sometimes, nothing is ever good enough. This attitude permeates our society and we have learned to complain about the smallest things. We are spoiled in so many ways. How did it get to this? Because we *can* complain, we *do* complain. This is one of the beautiful things, and also one of the ugly things about our society. That we have rights and can for the most part fully express our joy, anger, disgust, displeasure or any other feeling. We can do this all the way from a humble hamburger stand for the way the meat is cooked, to the White House for the way our country is run. Those are privileges we have because of immeasurable sacrifices on many fronts, and because of a pioneer attitude that was once a respected way of life. But we went overboard, and we lost our Balance and as a result we are losing our Power. But there is a bigger issue that has to do with the way we see ourselves. This whole caterwauling thing has transformed us into a culture of blame, loss of self-respect and worse, a loss of personal responsibility. The examples I refer to above are minor everyday occurrences that are relatively meaningless when taken by themselves. The bigger issue is that the culture of whining has transformed our society in a fundamental way.

Nothing is ever good enough, much less perfect.
It is always someone else's fault.
Why me? It is a pity party.
If only you could have done this differently.
It's not my fault...Poor me.
Stop me if you have never heard these everyday comments. It seems that at some time or another we all succumb to this escape, this weakness, this Surrender. This may be the worst manifestation of the loss of Power and Balance. It is also a form of Surrender. In this form of Surrender, we are not responsible for anything, not even for ourselves. Think about the self-

sufficient "Puritan Ethic" and the original Spanish and French settlers; the strength and attitude of those brave souls that settled our country from East to West. Compare that sufficiency and integrity to the modern-day legal system that tells us and has incorrectly taught us that everyone else is to blame. We have gone from "the buck stops here", to "I accept no responsibility." It is akin to pleading for the mercy of the court because you are an orphan, after having murdered your parents.

It is true that many times outside forces perhaps beyond our control, will be the cause of some injury or calamity. But even in those cases, Balance and Power will guide you through the difficult path and to Reconciliation. It seems so much easier to Surrender to whining, than to stop, listen, and acknowledge through honesty and Purity of Intent that we may be responsible, and that in any event perhaps we should make ourselves responsible, nonetheless. Imagine the Power one can derive from this practice!! Taking control and responsibility, especially when one is not required to do so. I view volunteerism as an example of this. How about risking your life in order to save another person's life? It is an example of selflessness and Purity of Intent.

Nobody likes a caterwauler.

Have you ever asked someone "what's wrong?"; "Tell me what's bothering you." Most of the time we ask that question somewhat innocently and not expecting an hourlong diatribe. But then the other person proceeds to rant incessantly about every little thing and detail about their problem or situation. Even if you may be asking sincerely and may care profoundly about this person's situation, we cannot escape or deny the eventual feeling of wanting to say "Ok, that's enough, stand up; suck it up; grow up and be bigger than the problems." "Take responsibility!" In prison that trait was a rare one indeed. Imagine how our world and lives would be permanently, profoundly, and basically altered if we all took responsibility for things we are responsible for and stopped caterwauling. This requires honest
self-analysis and Reconciliation. This is not to be confused with
self-punishment or self-flagellation. Those attitudes are not healthy and are destructive.
"I'm the worst!"
"I'm not worthy!"
No! That's not healthy reconciliation or self-analysis. That's self-recrimination. Instead imagine that one can calmly and confidently accept responsibility.

"I would not have lost my job if I had respected my employer's time."

"I would not have divorced, if I had been faithful."

"I would not have a DUI if I had not ignored the law."

"I would not have gone bankrupt if I had been more prudent."

"I would still have that friendship if I had not spoken ill of them."

"I wouldn't have lost control of my vehicle if I hadn't been talking on the phone."

This type of reconciliation sounds very similar to a confession in the Catholic faith, only it's not in the confessional. It is a spiritual experience to be able to do this in a strong, confident and positive manner. In fact, whatever Balance and Power was lost by the activity or event, can be not only restored, but strengthened by this practice. And it can be done at any time. The wonderful thing about this is that it is just you reconciling with yourself and by yourself.

Who has Power and Balance? You do...

Let us now practice this on a daily basis. It is difficult because it is anathema in our current society. One positive act at a time, however small, will change your life. Change others by example. Share your Balance and Power.

Who Are You, Really?

*A look in the mirror...do you dare see
yourself in others?*

14

WHO ARE YOU, REALLY?

When you take a moment to stop and think, to contemplate how we even exist in this universe, you stand in awe and wonderment at the incalculable miracle that has manifested itself in our existence. Simply from a biological perspective, the odds of you existing in this human form as a conscious, thinking and self-aware being, are improbable. It is not impossible obviously, because you exist, but improbable, nonetheless. Think for a moment. As we have discussed already, in order for you to exist you have to fight with and beat millions of spermatozoa to the ovum. Once there, you must be the first to successfully penetrate the ovum wall, and by that time you must have been exhausted. But you keep going until you finally make it through, And it's a good thing because once you got through, the ovum wall creates a barrier that prevents the millions of others that were wanting to meet their goal of entering the ovum. But you made it through first and they didn't. The ovum is now fertilized; it proceeds to create a unique one of a kind creation; the only one in the world; a unique **you**. It is a miracle that you exist.

I wonder, what might any one of them, or each and every one of those other potential persons have looked like or been like? What kind of life would they have had? I also think about their Purpose. After all they were alive and struggling to survive; perhaps that was their Purpose; but *you* were the one who survived against incalculable odds; selected for your unique life. You are the one who made it! How incredibly special. Now consider that this creation of you is the result of one event where you even had the chance to compete. Just one sexual act of perhaps thousands in the lives of your parents, which presented all of the conditions necessary for you to have a chance! You begin to recognize the numerical improbability of your existence.

Again, now consider that each of your parents faced the same incalculable odds of existence, but now multiplied by trillions of preceding events. If you take this process back into history to the origins of your ancestors, you recognize that your existence is so improbable, it is a miracle. And yet it happened. Here you are. A special creation. The only one of you in all of time, existence and in all of the Universe.

We sometimes, and perhaps most times, forget this because we live in a frenzied world, full of uncertainties, and populated by billions of other persons. The existence of so many billions of other humans seems to have a tendency to demean the value of another person, of each and every other creation sitting next to you on the bus, train, at the restaurant, office or football game.

"Well, they just aren't like me. They are so different. Look at the way they act and talk. And look at the way they dress!" Why is it that we always want others to conform to us? Can you imagine this world if we were all identical? Can you imagine a world and society where we all looked exactly alike, thought the exact same thoughts, behaved in the same manner, dressed exactly alike, had the exact same method of speech and expression? Where there were no distinguishing differences between us? A world of robots and artificial intelligence? There would be no unique *you* in that world. There would be no innovation or change. There would be no panoply of variations in culture, traditions, languages and the ways of life we treasure. We pay thousands of dollars to travel to see people and places because they are different. And so, we pretend to appreciate the differences in others, but secretly ask why they are the way they are. Did you ever think that others view you with those same eyes, the same questions and the same opinions?

Oh, the gift that God would give us, to see ourselves as others see us

If you have lots of things, you see those who have less or perhaps nothing, in a different way. If you have very little you see those that have much, as being very different. "I have a college degree; how could he not even graduate from high school?" It seems there is always suspicion about others. Successful people many times see others as lazy and unmotivated. Blue collar workers may see executives and businesspeople as unethical and thieves. In each person's mind, there is always a reason "those people" are *where* they are and *who* they are, and many times it is not a justified view. But Perspective is a powerful character in our lives.

Did you ever think that the working person is realizing their goal and may be very satisfied in life with the love of family and health, and without the Mercedes and the mansion? Did you ever think that the wealthy person who owns the company has a desire to accomplish a life's goal and that her invention changed the world? What do we really know about what is in the mind of another? We don't, and so we judge. What we find when we take the time to actually sit and talk to someone who seems so different, is that we really are very similar. We would learn that there are loves, fears, desires, goals, depression, struggles to survive and plain human nature that binds us and makes us very similar, if we would stop and learn about others. There is a treasure in them too. Every life is so unique, that each life is also a treasure.

We just took a different path. But that person was as successful as you in the race for existence. They made it. You made it. You both made it.

When we think about who we are, really, we must embrace who others are, in order to discover the answer.

Look at another as if you were looking in a mirror in order to reveal yourself to you

This must be done with Purity of Intent and without deception. What we discover is that we are all bound by the commonality of Existence. While that Existence and those interests may be manifested at different levels, they are very similar. This is empathy. This is acceptance and understanding at a level of Enlightenment. This is seeing a Creator within another being. The differences do not justify the behavior or thoughts that adversely affect our world in the form of war, class hatred, racism and discrimination in all its forms. So, who are you, Really?

You are that other person. ***En Lak Ech... You are my other self.*** Perhaps you took different paths after birth, but you share the same birthright. When you learn that you are not better or worse, you create adhesion and bind yourself to another unique and singular creation. That will give you Balance. And when you are in Balance, you are Powerful. This is an example of Balance in the world.

Compliments of Abraham Lincoln *cont.*

BALANCE

YOU CANNOT BRING ABOUT PROSPERITY

BY DISCOURAGING THRIFT;

YOU CANNOT STRENGTHEN THE WEAK

BY WEAKENING THE STRONG;

YOU CANNOT HELP THE WAGE EARNER

BY PULLING DOWN THE WAGE PAYER;

YOU CANNOT FURTHER THE BROTHERHOOD OF MAN

BY ENCOURAGING CLASS HATRED;

YOU CANNOT KEEP OUT OF TROUBLE

BY SPENDING MORE THAN YOU EARN;

YOU CANNOT BUILD CHARACTER AND COURAGE

BY TAKING AWAY MAN'S

INITIATIVE AND INDEPENDENCE;

YOU CANNOT HELP MEN PERMANENTLY,

BY DOING FOR THEM WHAT THEY COULD,

AND SHOULD, DO FOR THEMSELVES

Atributed to - Abraham Lincoln

Forgiveness

The enemy of pride

15

FORGIVENESS

It seems that Redemption and Forgiveness go hand in hand and that one is not possible without the other. It is almost as if the one results in the other. Redemption brings Forgiveness and Forgiveness results in Redemption. The two are tied together inextricably, dependent on each other as if in some mystical eternal dance. Both Redemption and Forgiveness are products of another consciousness; of a far different level of Being than we experience in our everyday normal selves. The goal is to transcend the shackles and boundaries of physical humanity. In physical being-ness, if you will, we are bound to billions of years of DNA, history, experience, culture, tradition and programming. It is difficult, and some would say, impossible to transcend what has come to be known as "human nature" or the "human condition." It is in our nature now in this time and in this place, to simply be the way we are. In other words, we are conditioned; we are trained. But what is it to be human and what is it to transcend human nature? Darwin would argue that our present human condition is the result of millions of years of natural selection; of "successful" evolution. The word itself, evolution, seems to indicate that we are evolved. Well, we have evolved into something. An alien being would wonder what exactly that evolution might be, if anything at all. The question is "what have we evolved into?" Into what exactly have we evolved as a species? Into what has each of us evolved as an individual being. Even the word "Being" is the progressive tense of the infinitive "to be." So as living entities, we are simply "being?" We are. It is reminiscent of the "I AM" in the Old Testament's name for "He who has no name", that being Yahweh, the God of the Hebrews.

And it is an appropriate joining of the two because when we realize who we really are, who others really are, that the Supreme Being, the God entity, "*It*" and all other forms in the universe, carbon based or not, animate or inanimate, recognizable or not, are all connected by a common origin of *oneness*, we begin to lift ourselves above the bondage of mere physicality. Most of the great religious teachings in history, from the Tao Te Ching and the Bible, to the Koran, Bhagavad Gita and others, have as one of their goals, to teach us to leave our bodies and to pass into spirit while on earth, so as to prepare us for Enlightenment. Black Elk of the Lakota Sioux wrote that when he was standing on the highest mountain of them all...,

"I saw more than I could tell,
and I understood more than I saw,
for I was seeing in a sacred manner the shapes of all things in the Spirit,
and the shape of all shapes as they must live together like one Being."

This was a transcendent experience. Black Elk left his body and experienced Enlightenment, while still a physical being. This happens. This is not an unknown or perhaps even a rare occurrence. While one could argue that he was able to experience this because he had a gift, I believe that you too can develop and learn to have these transcendent experiences if you surrender yourself to the Eterniverse. You must know and believe that this is possible in your life. You must simply start the process of being aware and having a "listening" for it. It is also interesting that we use the word "condition" in human condition. It could be argued that we are conditioned to react, behave, believe, retaliate and defend. Or it could be said that we are in a "condition" that has pejorative overtones.

I once believed that we should "accept the human condition and work within its framework." I have come to realize that working within its framework is only the foundation for helping us to realize a higher form of self, a more evolved and transcendent path to Enlightenment in ourselves and in others.

So, what does all this have to do with Forgiveness and Redemption? The metamorphosis that is either the result or the cause of Redemption in our physical lives is what we search and yearn for. Forgiveness and Acceptance are the sustenance that help it to reveal itself in our lives. In the movie *Gran Torino*, the old irascible character played by Clint Eastwood can find no value in any person or thing other than that with which he is familiar and accepts or that with which he agrees. He is myopic in his world views and critical of all else. He is a bigot, insulting and has reason to denigrate others who are unlike him. He is the manifestation of the human condition. But then a curious thing happens. Slowly, grudgingly, he begins to understand more about the Asians who surround him in his neighborhood. And in his own gruff manner, he starts to communicate with them and accept them as persons. Eventually, he comes to embrace them and defend them, eventually confronting their own adversaries and dying in the process. You could feel the transformation, the metamorphosis, from " human condition" to Enlightenment. It is a message of the Redemption of the human soul which transforms itself into Spirit and transcends this physical world.

Schindler's List is a difficult but uplifting story of the possibilities of our ability to transform. In Schindler's List, a mercenary business man, solely interested in profit, becomes the caretaker of persecuted and helpless Jewish prisoners, and eventually uses his position, power and money to save as many as he can, and when confronted with the fact that he could have saved more by giving the last of his possessions; a watch or lighter or some piece of jewelry, he recognizes his guilt and the fallacy of possessions and collapses in grief at the thought of his neglect and choices. What could have been. He weeps for those he could have saved but did not. He is cleansed. And so, Forgiveness and Acceptance are the precursors to Redemption. But it is not only the Forgiveness and Acceptance of others that brings us to Redemption, it is the Forgiveness of ourselves that also brings us to Redemption. This cannot be underestimated.

We cannot come to Redemption, to liberation, without first acknowledging and Forgiving ourselves. Surrendering to the Spirit gives you peace. In a truthful self-reconciliation, you cleanse yourself of the pain and guilt of your condition. We resist it because we are conditioned to believe and justify that our acts and thoughts are defensible. We couldn't possibly be wrong! You may very well know the Truth. But is it not a noble endeavor to seek another possible reality? Acceptance and Forgiveness can be realized through self-inquiry and Reconciliation. What a novel thought that we can Forgive ourselves through self-Reconciliation and even Forgive another. Remember how powerful Conscience, Perspective and Justification are.

I forgive you

We say that as some sort of celestial proclamation! Almost as if that person is not absolved unless you say so. Unless, I forgive you, you are not pardoned. It is my pardon that you need...The Camp commander in Schindler's List started pardoning prisoners because Schindler convinced him that having the power to pardon was greater that having the power to kill.

Where did we get the power and authority to forgive another? We perceive someone has harmed us; therefore, we have the power and authority to forgive them? When we pronounce forgiveness on another, are they really forgiven? Or is the offense still intact? Does your Forgiveness really make the offense and their guilt go away? Perhaps we say we forgive in order to make us feel better. Maybe Forgiveness is in not judging to begin with. In not adjudging that person as guilty of an offense against you. Perhaps Forgiveness lies not in us, but in them. In that quintessential "fifth **paradigm**" of universal oneness, where we are all part of the other.

I am always amazed at the dichotomy of our claimed beliefs versus our actual behavior. Jesus Christ taught his followers to "love your enemies." It is a basis upon which Christians claim to live their lives in faith. We have all seen and perhaps experienced the anguish of suffering relatives and loved ones at the trial of a murdered person. A loved one taken from us by a gruesome act of murder or desecrated by rape. At trial's end, when given the podium, the survivors say "I just want him to suffer. He deserves to experience the same pain he put my mother through. I hope he rots in prison. He deserves to die!!"

Interestingly, it is at trials where we seek punishment even though we preach forgiveness. Other examples of hypocritical comments people make regarding Forgiveness are "I forgive, but I don't forget" and "I forgive you, but God will get you." What kind of Forgiveness is that? I submit to you that such thinking is not Forgiveness at all, but merely a superficial feel good statement. It is much like Pontius Pilate washing his hands of the issue.

I am not saying that it would be easy to say the opposite. To say "I don't understand why this was done, but I believe in Redemption, Salvation and Acceptance and as painful as it is for me now, we cannot lose two lives. What can we do to transcend this loss and pain to transform another?" There are many uplifting accounts of those who have done just that. Of people who embraced the killer, sought reconciliation and changed lives by not living in Darkness, and by living in the Spirit of Light. As we evolve into more spiritual beings and leave behind the Darkness, little by little we begin to see the transcendence of Redemption, Forgiveness and Acceptance.

The practice of these principles gives you Balance and Power while on this Earth. The Tao to Enlightenment is within your grasp if you step outside the human condition and embrace that which by all arguments, is not part of human nature.

Live in the Light.

Abandon the Darkness.

Be an instrument of wondrous change in this Universe. It starts with one thought and one act. Be the strong one and act with brave compassion. Make it your actions that change the world.

A Look in the Mirror

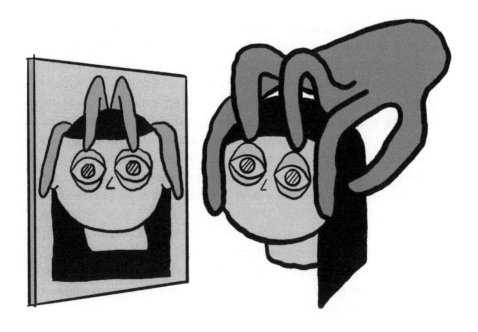

What do you really see?

16

A LOOK IN THE MIRROR

We look at things all day, every day. But what do we really see? This unbelievable gift of eyesight is one we take for granted. When you wake up and open your eyes, your first blurred images remind you that you can look at things. We go through the day and never really notice what it is we are looking at. That is because we are looking but not seeing. It takes effort to really see things and people.

In the morning when you stand in front of your mirror and get yourself ready in whatever form that takes, you are proceeding to change your appearance; make-up, hair, eyelashes, lipstick, false teeth, toupee, clothing, jewelry, footwear and other accoutrements. Why do we do this? Why do we have the need and desire to change our real and natural appearance? You will not look the same in a few transforming minutes. It is as if there are two distinct people from 6:00 am to 7:00 am. Think for a moment of all the things you do to transform your appearance, whether you are man or woman. What an obsession this is. So powerful is this activity that we dare not go out in public without appearing to be something we are not. So, what do people see when they look at you and you at them. Do we see the real person, or do we see only a facade? Imagine a world where the façade is unimportant. A world where your personal essence is what really matters. We talk about that, but we don't have the courage to live that way. The world is too judgmental. So, we succumb to the ritual and keep playing along, nobody really seeing and enjoying the real you or the real and authentic *me*.

I have always marveled at the ritual I undertake every morning when I go out into the world. In a very real sense, we are putting on our weapons of war. Getting ready for the daily battle. Yes, it's all about looking nice, attractive, strong and powerful. In fact, we even have names like "power ties and suits" and we put on our armor to do battle. Everything we do in that ritual, from our hairstyles and make-up, to our deodorant and clothing are designed to provide us with an edge; with better armaments for the day's activities. And you can't let up. At the first opportunity, we buy better clothes and nicer jewelry. Let no one see what's underneath! This is who I am. This is what I am. What you see is what you get...well, that's not quite true. Drill down past the mirage and see what you find. Perhaps you'll find a real person, including yourself.

At day's end we head home and try to relax. We try to leave all the day's activities and just forget that day's battle. So, what is the first thing we want to do? Shed all that armor we no longer need; those clothes that are so constricting. I want to put on some sweats and a t-shirt. I want to just be me. I don't need to impress anyone at this moment. That is when you become "real" again. Unfiltered by any requirement to impress or perform, we become just us, the real us. The one people should get to know.

Damn! The neighbor just knocked at the door! Oh! And look at me, I'm a mess...and here we go again. What an interesting and curious habit we have developed. Our reliance on things superficial in an attempt to define us. Ancient and Native cultures used war paint to define their ferocity. It may sound like I abhor or at least disdain this very human activity. Actually, all we have done is enhance with artificial means, what the animal kingdom has done for millions of years. When we are seeking a partner or hunting for success in life, we use the tools we must, in order to be successful in those efforts. Perhaps what we do to appear different, better, stronger and more likable is natural after all in a very strange way. Perhaps it's a natural act enhanced by artificial means.

In our increasingly artificial and superficial society, it is actually very interesting to observe. But the underlying question isn't how we look at ourselves and at things, but rather, how we "see" ourselves and other things. Let's peel away the layers of facade and see what we discover. Think about all of the clothing, uniforms, alterations, make-up, colors, armor and other appearances that we utilize today and that have been used in the history of humans.

Native American warpaint and headdresses;
A Judge's wardrobe
The garments of religious clergy and nuns
Japanese Samurai war apparel
A woman's executive business suit
Hair coloring to get rid of grey hair
Toupees or wigs
A man's power tie
Those new and popular Nike's
The traditional clothing of the Amish
Those ubiquitous tattoos.
Police uniforms
Baseball caps

Do you get the idea? Every one of these brings an image to mind. They all create an identity. Again, it is not a bad thing. It is just interesting to note how we identify ourselves by unnatural means. These are all designed to define and identify us; to give us an individual identity. In some cases, these identifiers are designed to gain advantage. It could be said that they are our "Public armor." I am always amused by people who want to be different by emulating something someone else is already doing.

Why is it public armor? Because we don't need them when we are alone or in private. In a very real sense, we are hiding the real self from the outside world. Imagine a totally passive and spiritually sick, rural person dwelling in old Japan. Then suddenly when called to service, this very same calm natured person transforms his appearance into a vicious fighter who is dressed in a uniform designed to frighten and paralyze the opponent. The Samurai. Fast forward to the twenty first century. A businessman arises from sleep and immediately starts the transformation from cuddly husband to relentless pursuer of the daily deal. Both are dressing for wars of different types.

It starts simply enough with a shower, then progresses to the selection of the armor of the day including that Hart Schaffner and Marx suit, the power tie, and don't forget the latest in stylish shoes. All the elements designed to impress, and in many ways to intimidate "the opponent." The Public Armor. At day's end when the battles are done, people shed the armor and return to being just regular likeable people.

The problem is that we can come to not only believe that we are those people we are dressed as, but embrace that character, much to our detriment. Again, it is not necessarily an undesirable thing. It's simply important to know and understand what is happening so that we do not become obsessed with the transformed personality. Equally as important in understanding others, is to see through the armor to the real person residing under it. Just to know that there is a human being under that armor that is there ostensibly to protect them. This helps us in relationships and communication, the listening to others as we interact. You can now have the experience of getting to know such a person in a different setting. You see the high-powered executive in a business meeting, and you establish an opinion based on her or his attire, behavior and speech. This image is well developed to gain advantage. It is important to note that the mannerisms and vocabulary and their method of delivery are also part of the public armor. Now fast forward and you happen to spend some private, quiet and nonpublic time with this same person and small, almost imperceptible things start to happen when they are not on the stage performing.

First, he loosens his tie then he relaxes his speech and starts to talk like a "normal" person. He smiles and maybe leans back into his chair and lets down his public persona. He is taking off his public armor. And your mind reacts and says, "This guy isn't anything like I thought he was." You get past the facade and get to know the real person and you start to connect and maybe even become friends.

The next time you see this same person in a public setting, guns a blazing, you know that there is another person behind the armor, and you appreciate that person in a very different way because you saw the person without the public armor.

Things are not what they seem. Not with things, not with events, not with problems and not with people. Understanding this phenomenon is important to having Balance and Power in your life and relationships.

Now let us move on to our own view in the mirror. How do we see ourselves? How *can* we see ourselves?

Right now, I want you to go to a mirror in the privacy of your home, office or other quiet, private place where you will not be interrupted. This is preferably done at home, in your dress down clothes with none of your armor on including jewelry or make-up. Go to the mirror now and look at yourself. Stare at yourself. Now I want you to see what you are looking at. **Look into your eyes deeply without looking away.** Do this for at least one minute. Don't look away. This is what other people don't see. This is even what you don't see because you don't take the time to see yourself.

What do you see?
Who do you see?
Is that person familiar?
Are you angry at that person?
Do you see a warrior?
Do you see self-doubt?
Are you embarrassed?
Do you see fear?
Can you forgive that person?

Perhaps you see pride or maybe confidence. Some people see a hurting person full of fear, shame, guilt and embarrassment. Whatever you see, this is a good time to acknowledge the feeling of who and what you see. If you see something that surprises or even scares you, understand that you are peeling back the layers that obfuscate, that hide you from yourself and others. We resist this knowing of ourselves because we need a secret place where no one ever goes and no one will ever know, not even you. It can be frightening!!

We resist seeing and understanding ourselves because it is difficult to accept that perhaps we really aren't the person, the being, that we pretend and want to be both to ourselves and to others. Looking, then seeing into your own soul and understanding who and what you are is the beginning of releasing the shackles of the facade and the public armor. This gives you Power to be the spiritual being you seek to be, and the Balance of now understanding and seeing through your own armor and the armor others use to hide themselves. But understand that they are, and you are, hiding behind the armor.

Understand who and what you are today. Reconcile. Practice. Breathe the Spirit into yourself. Enthéos is God Within. Seek the path that leads you to co-existence with Enlightenment. You will find Peace, Balance and the Power of Everything.

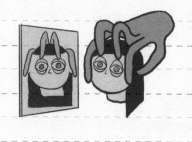

Reconciliation

Make peace with the Universe

17

RECONCILIATION

From Funk and Wagnalls new Encyclopedia:

To Restore to friendship after estrangement
To bring to acquiescence
To make or show to be consistent or congruous
To adjust the differences or inconsistencies in...
To restore to sacred uses and to be in communion with...

I will add my definition:

"To make Peace with the Universe"

The Universe/Eterniverse includes everything physical that exists today, existed in the past and will ever exist in the future. That is a lot to Reconcile. That is a lot to think about. So, let's think about Reconciliation in a different way in this discussion. Settling your accounts, so that they are straight. When we think of Reconciliation in a local and personal sense, we think of Reconciliation as it relates to our relationships with other human beings. In that reespect, it is not physical, but spiritual.

By way of example, when a husband and wife are estranged and then decide to re-join, they are considered reconciled. The same may be said of parents and their children, brothers and sisters, business partners and estranged friends, all when they decide to lay down their swords of aggressiveness and the shield and armor of protection.

Acquiescence is also a form of Reconciliation. You give up your position to another and "acquiesce" in a non-confrontational manner. In this case, there may not be a re-joining, but instead a simple nod to the other whether verbal or in a physical acknowledgment that says, "I understand your position." My original mentor said that in love, war and business there were things that were understood, but unspoken. I didn't understand that until much later in life when I had much more experience. Indeed, there are things that are not spoken but understood by all parties involved.

Reconciliation also takes the form of a search for consistency in things. How can we Reconcile that high-level executives in Corporate America earn 400 times more than their employees? It doesn't seem consistent; it seems incongruous. It is as they say, "non sequitur". It doesn't follow, somehow. I can't get my arms around the concept that there could be so much of a difference or inconsistency in their respective compensation. I just can't Reconcile that fact. That doesn't mean it can't be reconciled.

Also, Reconciliation can be a means, a Táo or Path, to restoring something sacred and thus to be in communion with that sacred entity, thought, concept, relationship or person. It makes sense and in fact we feel exhilaration and Peace that is almost uncontainable when we Reconcile. When we Reconcile in these ways, we feel elation and a sense of freedom from the chains of separation, fear and shame.

But how is this so? What is this feeling and why do we experience it?

It feels like a selfless act of sharing; like the acceptance of rigor and discipline; Like sacrificing for someone because you love them enough to abandon your own self-interests for them and to them; like the incomparable light of Enlightenment and seeing something sacred in another person and being in selfless communion with them. Imagine that you have the opportunity to experience this Reconciliation with others. Now imagine that there is an opportunity to Reconcile with your other self, your inner, hidden and unknown self, every day! Imagine that you can Reconcile every event in your day before you retire for that day.

Remember that look in the mirror? There is an Enlightened Being, another Divine Spiritual Entity inside of you, in your Mind and in your Spirit. This is the inner voice that speaks to you constantly, every hour of every day. A voice that you may not be listening to is quite a different matter, but it does speak to you if you but have a listening for it.

The Catholic Church has as one of its Sacraments, the Sacrament of Reconciliation. It is commonly known and referred to as confession, which in my opinion is a gross misstatement and misunderstanding of what Reconciliation really is. My non-Catholic friends almost always refer to Catholic confession in derogation, and as one of their most visceral alienations of the Catholic dogma. Their comments are almost identical, word for word, "Why should I confess my sins to a man, any man? A man cannot forgive my sins. I will not confess my sins to any man!"

Understood. That is fair enough. It is interesting however that it does in fact acknowledge that there is a concept and acknowledgement of sin and that there are sins to be confessed. Without delving into specific dogma of the Catholic Church, and while I only occasionally go to confession, I understand the argument. But I must also say that the argument misses the point. It ignores the real value and benefit of the process. The point is not that you are confessing to another human, nor that you seek forgiveness from that person (you aren't). The point is that you are Reconciling to yourself. You are opening your heart and soul and releasing the pain, guilt, agony, hurt and shame that you have been holding inside, as painful as that may be. That example just happens to be in a confessional. But in my non-dogmatic and non-religious view for which I am criticized, it doesn't have to be that way. It does not have to be in a confessional at all. It can be in your home at night before you go to bed. It can be in your office or place of business. It can be while you are driving. In fact, in the purest and simplest sense, *you yourself are the confessional.* A Reconciliation can only take place when you are present and aware that you are reconciling an issue. You need to Release…

You have seen it play out on television when a suspect is being questioned by the police or an interrogator. At first, the suspect denies and objects and even gets angry that they would ever consider that he did the crime. This back and forth goes on and on and it seems that it will never end. Eventually, after thinking for a while about what he did, he starts talking and can't stop. It spills out because he couldn't hold it in any longer. He couldn't help himself. He had to confess to it even if it doomed him. There is that whole conscience thing going on again.

Think for a moment that you have a certain something (some might call it a sin) that you are hiding that bothers you. It is on your mind and it is giving you feelings of guilt, shame or simply discomfort. It isn't settling quite right with you and you wish there was someone you could talk to; someone you could share it with to get it off your mind. Someone whom you could trust and who wouldn't judge you, but who would just listen. You go to that person and for all intents and purposes, you "confess" this certain something. You talk and explain. You give reasons and share your feelings. You Rationalize from your Perspective. You spill your guts. We have all done this. Did you let it all out? Do you remember the freedom you felt? You felt liberated. You confessed!!

You set things straight by talking to another man or woman or perhaps a child. You restored yourself and perhaps acquiesced. You adjusted inconsistencies and came to terms with your sacred inner self. You were in communion.

Now I submit to you that you can self-Reconcile every night before you go to sleep. But in this self-Reconciliation I ask you to Reconcile by yourself and for yourself, with your Sacred inner self and directly with the God Within. You will not believe the Liberation and Power and Peace this generates in you. It is no less than an act of purification.

This is not an exercise in self-recrimination. It is an act of cleansing. It is a process of looking into yourself, and discussing any issue that is unsettled, however difficult that issue might be that remains unreconciled in your day and in your life. When I do this, I may actually be talking as if I were communicating with another entity. It is because I am. I worry little, if at all, that someone might consider me a bit crazy. It is this communication and communion with your Sacred inner self and the God Within that restores you from your own estrangement from yourself; the self-punishment and self-flagellation. It adjusts all of the little or seemingly big inconsistencies in your life's day, and gives you Peace, Strength and Balance. More than that, it gives you inner Vision and a deep and truthful understanding about you, that only you are best equipped to provide.

It is difficult for me to express in frail words the immense Power and Peace this invites into my life and into my soul. It is a liberating and inspiring, personal and spiritual experience.

In this process, your Mind is cleansed.
In this process, your Spirit is purified.
You Reconcile yourself to your Sacred inner self.
The Power is in you. Peace is with you. You are in Communion with your Entheos; Your God Within.

Eternity

There is only "now", and even that is gone before you can grasp it...

18.

ETERNITY

I am watching; I am enjoying and seeing my friend paint a portrait of a figure that is important to him. He is putting on canvas an image that exists now and only in his mind. I believe, as does he, that because he creates this image from his mind and paints it, he must expect it will live into the future. Perhaps Forever. He wishes that his ideas and thoughts will be manifested in his art, and for that art to live in the minds of others. Otherwise, why would he be painting it? It must last and it must live; it must communicate to those who do not know him, well after he and his subject are gone. In our current scope of understanding of time and space, his art may last for many future generations to see and enjoy. It is a wonderful representation of someone he knows and loves. His work lives now and he hopes it continues to live Forever...Perhaps for all Eternity in the future.

It has always been a source of wonder to me that people can have a thought in their mind whether it is an image that can be manifested in painted or sculpted art, sounds that can be made into music and a symphony or numbers and calculations that can be developed into mathematical equations that are indecipherable to most people. Shakespeare's Hamlet is reflecting admiringly and despairingly in the monologue, as he says,

"What a piece of work is man!"

Hamlet was commenting on the human condition; however, I prefer to interpret that phrase in a sense of amazement and awe of what humanity can be. What an amazing creation we are. Each of us is a special creation, whether you believe it or view it from a religious, spiritual or scientific perspective. Either way, we are a very special piece of work irrespective of how we got here. We are a "once in the Eterniverse" creation. That is a long time. Eternity is a long time. The interesting thing about eternity in time and space and the infinity of numbers we rely on to express time and space, is that there was a past eternity that no longer exists, a future eternity that doesn't yet exist and most shockingly, a present "now" that is existing forever at this very moment. So, in a very real sense, the only eternity we really have and can ever expect to have is right now, and even the "now" is already gone before you can grasp it. This whole concept of eternity and how we ended up in it is quite puzzling. Really... how do you get out of Eternity? Can you get out of Eternity?

Lovers in Love say, "I will love you forever." In the moment, it says and speaks that which is in the heart and soul. Forever is a long time. We speak those words with the emotion of the moment and for some, the emotion and commitment fade if not entirely, at least in intensity. What do they really mean? Forever is a long time. We are bound by time and space, in this life and in this existence. We don't see it readily, but we are bound by time and space. Bound...tied; unable to separate ourselves from them, like Prometheus. We can move, but our movements are limited by gravity and the limitations of a physical body. We age, but time moves at its own pace. Neither too quickly, nor too slowly. It just is. Time and space govern our physical existence. There is an old saying,

"All men fear time... but Time...? it fears only the pyramids".

It is a commentary on our existence as physical beings, albeit an engaging metaphor about our captivity by time and space with something with which we can easily relate; the Pyramids.

Most major religious beliefs make reference to an afterlife; that state of being or otherworldly existence that follows this physical and temporal life. While some beliefs tell us of an "Eternal" life after physical death, others tell us of a progression to a higher level of physical existence accompanied by a more highly acute spiritual enlightenment. It can all be very confusing because there are so many belief systems. That is why most people who find a religion they believe in just stay with one belief system or religion. However, studying other beliefs can place one on a path of discovery that can provide an understanding of other perspectives and beliefs in an afterlife and how they understand eternity. Another interesting human characteristic about the next eternal life is that all these beliefs are referenced in some form of physical existence. The images we have created of the afterlife are manifested in a physical place and human form. There are rarely manifestations of the afterlife in a non-physical form or place; such as Pure Spirit or Pure Energy. For us, in this physical plane, it is difficult to imagine something that has no physical form or place. Think about the references we make to eternity, its places and its residents.

The Right Hand of God
    The Heavenly Throne
        The Eternal City
            The New Jerusalem
                Up in the Heavens
                    The devil; Satan
                        Burning in Eternal fire

We live in the physical world and endeavor to explain eternity in a manner with which humans can relate. I submit to you that eternity has no time or space or location.

How about Reincarnation? Being physically re-born again in body; eventually transcending to Enlightenment.

The re-uniting of Mind and Body? In the afterlife, the spirit and Body re-unite after the physical death of the body. Additionally, we see all those who died before us, and enjoy their company for all eternity. I believe that in the search for Truth, it is important to think about alternative views of Eternity. Perhaps we want something we don't understand...Something that is not describable. The Greeks named a place called Utopia. We interpret that as meaning Paradise. But the word Utopia, when translated means "no place".

The ancient Greeks had a God of all Gods. His name was Zeus. (Deus, Dios). There were no Gods before him. All Gods, Demigods, Titans, Gorgons and mere human figures were subservient to Him. The intricately interwoven lives of the pantheon of Greek mythological characters all originated from, and fed into a Master Story, a Matrix that made sense of the physical world, to the general human Greek populace. Everything from agriculture and fire, to thunder and lightning was explained by the mythology and their wondrous stories. Modern disciplined thinkers have dismissed mythology as exactly that; a myth. Just a bunch of old-world unsophisticated people trying to explain the stars, fire, agriculture, the sun, life, death and the universe and life as we know it. Perhaps they shouldn't be dismissed so readily. The Greeks had a sense for time and space. They knew there were elements that could not be seen or measured, that could not be contained. So much so, that Zeus, the "Grand Master" the beginning of all life and time, the Original One, had his own beginnings in, of all things, his parents. Few people know this. Who were they? What were their names? How could they have existed Before Zeus?

In perhaps the greatest display and manifestation of the Greeks' understanding of the concepts of eternity, time, space and things unseen, the Greeks named them

CHRONOS > "TIME"   and   *CHAOS > "GAS" (SPACE)*

Chronos and Chaos were the parents of Zeus. Time and Space. We don't know why the Greeks were able to think in this evolved and sophisticated manner, but whatever the source of their enlightenment, they knew that the physical world was transcended by Time and Space. To them, these were Eternal elements that had no beginning. Whether due to intervention, or because of purely human enlightenment, the Greeks understood that our physical world was constrained, and that in the next dimension, it was governance over time and space, or perhaps the absence of time and space, that defined Eternity. Perhaps that is how we become freed from Eternity; where there is an absence of Time and Space.

I'm sure you have contemplated Time and Space. When you begin to understand the enormity of the Eterniverse, it is hard to understand *how* it exists and it is also equally difficult to understand *why* it exists. It is an unknown...

In the known universe, there are trillions of stars like our sun. There are some galaxies like our own Milky Way that have over a trillion stars just in that one galaxy. We are part of a local group of galaxies. There are countless galaxies in our cluster of galaxies; There are countless clusters in our super-cluster. There are countless super clusters in our region of the Universe... ad infinitum. Where does the universe end? When you reach that "end," would there not be an entire universe beyond that, perhaps not in our dimensional understanding, but a separate Universe, nonetheless? And beyond that, what is there? Something else? Nothing? Everything else?! That is why I call it the Eterniverse. If there is one more Universe, then there is an eternity of Universes. There is no end to space, time or numbers, at least as we know and understand them in this physical plane. Scholars have said that the Universe is 13.7 Billion years old. But in reality, the argument is that the Big Bang is 13. 7 billion years old. It does not ask the question, "what was the age of the Universe before the "Big Bang"? There is no age for the Eterniverse that can be attributed or imagined.

Have you considered how much time it takes to travel in space?

Our best-known reference is the speed of light, which is 186,282.397 miles per second. Supposedly, there is nothing in the Universe faster than the speed of light. This is our current understanding based on the physical conditions as we now understand them. That is really fast, but that means it takes one year, at that speed, for light to travel 5,898,788,599,814 miles!!! Our closest Star neighbor is over 4.24 light years away (Proxima Centauri). And that is our closest star neighbor! That means that it takes over four years for light traveling at 186,282.397 miles *per second* to reach us from there. That's 25 trillion miles distant, and it's our closest neighbor! It is difficult to comprehend such numbers and distance, and yet, those numbers are just the beginning of Eternity. It is as if Eternity hasn't even begun to show itself. Are you beginning to grasp the concept? It seems that fast as light can travel, in the scope of the Eterniverse, it travels very slowly.

As humans, we try to control space and time much as we try to control everything else. To do so, we describe time in seconds, minutes, hours, days, weeks, months, years, decades, centuries and millennia. We describe space and distance in fractions of an inch, inches, feet, yards, miles and parsecs. A light year is an attempt to describe space and time. But space and time are not measurable. So, what is Eternity? Scientists posit countless theories about these unanswered questions.

Is it real? Was there a beginning? What was there before the beginning? Was there time before the beginning? What exists on the other side of the end of this universe? Is it imagined? Does the concept of Eternity only exist in our minds? Is it a purely human construct? Do animals have a sense of time and space? Does it matter to them?

It is part of the human condition to want to live forever. The body struggles to die. It wants to stay here. It wants to live, even if for just one more breath and even if you are not aware of it seeking that one more breath. As sentient beings, we can think about, and be aware of our existence. Descartes wrote: *I think, therefore I am..*

Because we can think and because we have a mind that creates thoughts, fears, hopes, wishes dreams and other nebulous concepts, we can also think about time, space and Eternity. If you can think, you can know that you exist. Just being aware that you exist is a really important part of our humanity. It is called Consciousness and Self Awareness. However, *now that you know that you exist*, you will then also need to ask, *"how did I come into existence?"*

"why do I exist and what is my purpose for being here in this particular time and place?"

"where will I go, if anywhere, after I no longer exist here", and

"how long will I exist in that place?"

"will there be consciousness or just pure energy?"

So, you see, we are always thinking about and wishing for that next place called Eternity. And if you stop and think about it, Eternity, even if it is a Paradise, can be pretty frightening!

Perhaps you will walk in a meadow and sit by a lake. There is no need for food, so you can't have that pizza, or hamburger or healthy salad. Maybe you will take a quiet walk in a forest; or maybe you will traipse in a field of flowers. Happy, skipping, walking, happy; lots of flowers, lots of fields...traipsing...you never get tired, you catch as many fish as you want, there are no challenges, there are no goals; there are no accomplishments or rewards; Forever...For all Eternity...It will never end. After all, how much traipsing can one do? I'm having fun, but how long do I have to be here?

When we ascribe human, physical and earthly attributes to Eternity, including time and space, yes, it could be frightening precisely because it would never end!! We create those human and physical images into Eternity because that is what we can understand and relate to. It gives us comfort, so we create it from a human Perspective. I submit to you that Eternity is not about the physical realm. Whatever the Eternity experience might be, it most certainly is not an existence that is bound by either Time or Space. In fact, Time and Space must be absent in such an existence. It is simultaneously instant and eternal. It is transcendent.

I Am now, for Eternity.

The Art of Inquiry and Listening

It is both art and science

19

THE ART OF INQUIRY AND LISTENING

One of the secrets that most successful people understand is the art of Inquiry. Just knowing the right conversation and questions. This is a whole new world that most people never discover and enjoy. But just what is this "Inquiry"? It sounds simple enough doesn't it? The first vision that might come to mind is that of an investigator like those we see on TV where they relentlessly interrogate the "suspect" into submission until the suspect just gives in, sometimes even if they aren't guilty. The true art of Inquiry is not the obtrusive practice that invades people's comfort zone. We have all known people who want to get into everyone's business. These people are basically nosey, busy bodies who want to know everyone's personal business. That kind of inquiry isn't really inquiry at all, but rather it is an obnoxious and personal affront that over a period of time can be destructive to relationships and can result in a loss of respect for the person who is just being intrusive. It is also not like an interview where there is an obvious barrier between people, whether that barrier is physical or imaginary. This kind of "interview" is too structured, mercenary, and is not conducive to the real art of Inquiry. To be true to Purity of Intent, one must honestly have the interests of another as the underlying motivation and basis of the conversation. However, this is not an easy exercise or effort. It is a lifelong learning process. Most of us are conditioned to serve ourselves before we serve others. It could be said that it is instinctive for us to see the benefit to ourselves first, before recognizing the benefit to others. I have learned that discovering what others want or how they would benefit leads you directly to the solution and answer. In a negotiation, most people do not want to hear what the other person wants, while that is precisely what you must discover in order to find common ground.

Inquiry and Listening. It is a melody so sweet that it enhances your clarity and sensitivity to newfound levels you never thought possible. This art form is more like a conversation that opens the mind to a free exchange of thought. A discussion. An exercise in learning the desires, motivations, fears, goals, threats and dreams of the person with whom this "thought exchange" takes place.

One of the obstacles to Listening is the Messenger and the manner and method of delivery. In ancient times, when the royal recipient of bad news opened and read the message, they would punish or kill the messenger.

Worse, the interpretation and manner of delivery rendered the actual message meaningless. Think of someone telling you something that is correct, but that they tell it to you in a way that is aggressive and judgmental. It makes you angry, you respond in like manner and the message, although it may have been correct, is lost due to the manner in which the message was delivered. Think again of a person who has been convicted of a crime who is a "known criminal". That person could make a factual statement to you, but you may not believe it because of the judgment you have of that person's past. Think again of a person of authority that is in a position of trust such as a boy scout leader, a pastor or the Governor of your state. That person could give you a message that is false in its entirety, but because of their position, you would believe the message. Listening goes beyond the person and the manner in which they deliver a message.

The art of Inquiry is based upon a sincere interest in the other person or phrased another way, in the other person's interests in a sincere manner. It is a process where one inquires as to the person's inner thoughts with simple, honest and sincere conversation as you would with a close and dear friend. Imagine your best friend who is troubled; Imagine a conversation with that best friend where you ask "Tell me what is on your mind. What is troubling you?". It is a simple question which will often yield a long response, revealing their inner thoughts, emotions, fears, desires or other feelings. If you listen carefully instead of speaking and giving advice, you will learn the answers and solutions to that person's issues. You will learn that when you listen people will open their hearts and mouths and proceed to tell you things you couldn't have imagined. It is shocking! Yet, you will learn to listen. This discipline is difficult to implement because we are trained by society to talk and *not* to listen. To give our "valuable" opinion. To talk over people in an effort and demand to be heard, because after all, you have something important to say. But when you do this you block incoming ideas and knowledge.

When you listen, something else happens that is truly amazing. The person with whom you are sharing this exchange, many times solves their own issues and arrives at self-evolved solutions!! I have experienced this hundreds if not thousands of times. It is awesome to experience and observe a person discover on their own, an answer or solution, and even think that you helped them arrive at the solution as they are thanking you for helping them. The reality is that you did help them because you asked a simple question or questions, you had a sincere conversation, you were sincerely interested and very importantly, you also just Listened. However, once again I repeat, this is a very difficult discipline. Why is that?

It is our human impulse to speak, to give advice, to interrupt, and in effect "not listen". Try this exercise and you will see how difficult it is. The next time you are in a deep conversation try to not speak for minutes on end. Focus on Listening intently on what the other person is saying. At appropriate intervals or pauses, respond solely with applicable comments like:

"I see"
"Tell me more
"Wow!! That's interesting".
"Why do you say that"?
"That's hard to believe!!"
"How do you feel about that"?
"Then what happened"?

While this may be an exaggeration, it makes a point that people want to talk if you let them and they'll tell you more than you'll ask, if you allow them to. This is not unlike a listening that a counselor might engage in with a client. The key is that like a counselor, you are listening for a pure reason and not for ulterior motives. Most people love to talk about their families, jobs/work and hobbies. These topics open up the conversation on a platform that is known as "Common Ground". You are both on Common Ground, at the same level, and can now commence the wonderful art of Inquiry and Listening.

Because 93% of communication is non-verbal, Listening is accomplished not solely through hearing, but through other more profound elements if the realm of listening. Listening includes

recognizing someone's split second micro facial expressions,
observing how they sit
watching how quickly they move or fidget
aggressive eye contact or avoidance of eye contact
eye movement
pausing before an answer
clearing of the throat
a smile or a frown
nervous laugh
a grimace
nervous foot tapping
the irregular sound and pitch of the voice or the voice drifting off
the eyebrows moving

head scratching
head pitching forward
wringing of the hands
all five fingertips touching the other fingertips
leaning back
leaning forward

There are countless others, but this gives you an idea how many elements contribute to Listening.

Successful people train themselves in this discipline. It is an art form that is learned over time with much practice, and when applied properly is a truly fulfilling experience. I refer to successful people not only as it relates to business, but most importantly how this can be an everyday experience for all of us in our personal lives. Successful in your meaning and purpose in life, not just in the attainment of "things".

EVERYBODY WINS

Much has been said and much has been written about "how to negotiate" a deal or a settlement or a final offer. We have this abiding image of the "tough as nails" negotiator and unfortunately, it is the one that most people relate to. This guy is almost our hero!!! ***You should see the deal he negotiated. He took him for all he was worth!!!*** This is akin to a form of warfare which is how most people and the average untrained person comprehend being a participant in such an exchange. It is a difficult, hard-nosed, almost "winner take all" exercise which is defined by having winners and losers. An interesting note is that the "winner" in these negotiations usually has advantages such as the power of an institution, government, reputation or wealth or some other form of power which supports them and even gives credibility to the "winner". They negotiate from a position of strength and not from a position of weakness.

I recall as a young businessman; I listened very carefully and learned a plethora of techniques to negotiate a deal. I was involved in literally thousands of these negotiations, many involving sales presentations I made of certain products I was selling at the time. I got really good at winning. I could negotiate anything, and for me the proof was in the concessions I literally extracted from people. It really was like warfare and I was very proud of how talented I had become in this so-called discipline. Today, it is glorified in the business world as Bushido, "the art of war".

The idea was to win at almost any cost. Take no prisoners. Then, many years later, a business associate of mine commented to me that if he ever needed to negotiate a deal, he wanted me on his side. He stated that if he "went to war" he would want to go to war with me on his side. I took it as a supreme compliment. Then he said something that changed me forever. He said, "but if you notice, some of the hardnosed deals you negotiate end up failing because you are too good. You are so good at it that you leave nothing on the table including the other person's self-respect. Leave something on the table and let people have some dignity when you're done". At the time I thought that such an approach was a sacrilege, especially in the business world. I lived in the world of "take no prisoners". However, I eventually realized that I had a lot to learn about the true discipline of negotiating, Inquiry and Listening.

I thought about this anathema over a long period of time and eventually I came to understand the power of a conversational exchange; the discussion, the Inquiry and the Listening. Because I respected his opinion, I started employing my business associate's philosophy even though it made me very uncomfortable at first. I asked myself why and how this could be a good thing? After all, weren't we trained to win at everything and to win everything? I soon learned the answer. It was a good thing because it provides a venue to enter into an agreement where everybody wins. And I discovered that in the end it was far more fun and most importantly, it was far more gratifying than my previous results. I had to discipline myself to Inquire as to what my "partner" in the negotiation wanted out of the deal. I had to attune myself sincerely to work toward a mutually beneficial result. To do this, I had to discover what my partner in the exchange desired for him or herself or their company. I had to listen..... instead of speaking and interrupting. I learned that when the conversation reveals what they want, you can then craft a solution that is mutually beneficial and acceptable out of the matrix of information you just received. Or in the alternative, one might discover that there is no deal there, at least not one that will last. There is nothing wrong with that result because it is an honest exchange that one can live with.

Most of the time, when I start such a conversation in a negotiation after conversing comfortably for a while, I will simply say "I want to share my thoughts with you about this and I want to ask you to share your thoughts with me about this as well. I really don't want to guess what you need and want, and I don't want to try to discover that by going through a long and uncomfortable series of negotiations, offers and counter offers and adversarial conversations.

You also should not have to guess what I need and want. I prefer instead that you inform me of what it is you want and need and what is important to you, and I likewise will do the same for you. When we are then both aware of each other's wants and needs and what is important to each of us, we will have a much better opportunity to craft an agreement that benefits us both. We'll know relatively quickly if there is something we will be able to do. Can you tell me what your thoughts are about this?"

THIS APPROACH GIVES YOU POWER!!!

I have utilized these forms of communication in areas from the purchase of commercial real estate to art. It's a balanced approach if it is based on Purity of Intent. But it must be genuine, and it cannot be just a contrivance where one is faking sincerity with the subliminal goal of only winning for oneself. Being genuine in your intent and approach is key to its success. It is exactly what gives you the Power. I assure you that people can sense and feel it.

I am always amazed and impressed at the look on people's faces when I approach a negotiation or conversation this way. Everyone drops their defenses and guard, and a genuine productive conversation is likely to result. It is a fair-minded approach where your partner believes that you want to enter into a fair and equitable agreement. I was also surprised that this approach allowed me to negotiate from an inferior position. I have literally just told people, "I need your help to get this done. I can't do this without you". It is amazing how people react to the honesty and openness. You find that people want to help. It is in our nature to want to help and reach solutions. In this process I have discovered that the most seemingly insignificant things are really important to people that you never would have known otherwise. You would have been deprived of the benefit of the honest and open conversation and the gratifying results.

So far, this discussion seems like an approach only as it relates to business. Personal issues can benefit from the arts of Inquiry and Listening as well. Relationships with spouses, children, brothers and sisters, parents and friends all involve discord or misunderstanding at some time or another. While I am reticent to refer to Reconciliation in these relationships as a negotiation, in a very real sense, Reconciliation is a negotiation as well. The same principles apply if the goal is to seek understanding and common ground with each other. I remember my father telling me "hablando, se entiende". Loosely translated it means "in speaking (communication) there is understanding", or "communication yields understanding". One of the reasons we resist communicating our innermost feelings, desires and needs is that we feel like it makes us weak, exposed and vulnerable, as if we were "giving it up and surrendering." That is understandable. We feel exposed to the potential onslaught of repercussions such as judgment by others or an insincere motive. But you will find that this kind of sharing can many times open the door for the other person to share as well. They too will engage in the communication and sharing as it transcends words and becomes an almost spiritual liberation. While this is not always successful, isn't it worth the effort to reconcile and understand each other? It is the sincere Inquiry with the goal of a mutually acceptable result based on Purity of Intent that can provide empowerment to all parties. This works if you listen, and really listen carefully, instead of thinking about what you are going to say next. That is the most difficult discipline because we are preparing to speak instead of listening. That's human nature. Another key is to avoid judgment of the situation or of the person with whom you are communicating.

Passing judgment and forming opinions changes the way you listen.

You start listening selectively, and it impairs your ability to enter into a sincere conversation based upon Purity of Intent. This doesn't mean that it is always a successful endeavor because it isn't always a success. But it gives you a real opportunity and the best chance to succeed based on mutual respect.

Inquiry to gain Power...

Listen to gain Balance...

Everybody wins

Build a Powerful Self

Yes; you have a choice

20.

BUILD A POWERFUL SELF

We have discussed several methods and approaches to gaining Balance and Power in your life in the face of a crazy and frenzied world. The goal is to develop your inner strengths in order to meet the challenges in the world and in the process gain Peace, Purpose and Power. This is a life-long effort. It takes commitment to yourself and it takes practice. The beautiful thing is that you can employ these principles wherever you may be and under almost any circumstance. The opportunities for growth are everywhere. To get to the core of these principles, we have discussed many ideas.

Purity of Intent	Forgiveness
Reconciliation	Surrender
Inquiry	Listening
Possessing things	The Truth
Inner Vision	Right and Wrong
Redemption	Eternity
Perspective	Justification
Conscience	Consciousness
The Brain and the Mind	The Mind and the Body
Virtue	Being Undefeatable
Giving and Receiving	

The goal is to engage in each of these values and concepts in an effort to develop Balance and Power in your life. To become a Powerful Self that is Undefeatable. Perhaps it is not a function of developing Balance and Power but rather discovering that you already possess these values and finetuning them to fit your unique life experience. Everyday life and daily experiences are all opportunities to grow.

It seems that for every value and virtue, there is a contravening idea or habit that fights us at every turn. It seems that the journey to almost any level of Enlightenment on this earth, in this physical life, is met with an opposing force. Nonetheless, it is an exciting, worthwhile, rewarding and euphoric journey. Like fine wine, we metamorphose from one state of being to another. Both are wondrous. The vine and the wine. Our basic humanity, like a grape, is a very beautiful, precious and wondrous state of being. It is, and we are. But there is no denying that the transformation to wine is also wondrous and a miracle to behold. It is as much a miracle as existence itself. So, we are on this path accompanied by this "noble struggle" to become Balanced and Powerful, and to have Peace and Purpose. For all things physical, there are spiritual counterparts.

For every Surrender, there is Triumph
For every prison, there is Liberation
For every insincerity, there is Purity of Intent
For every judgment, there is Reconciliation
For every hypocrisy, there is Truth
For every Death, there is Life Eternal
For every sin, there is Forgiveness
For every Doubt, there is Hope
For every shackle, there is a key

We are children of the Eterniverse. Therefore, we are all part of each other. We are all different and unique working and living parts of one grandiose organism made up of trillions of parts. We are one great wondrous living being.

So, can we do this? Is it possible to reach the seemingly other worldly state of being in this physical life? It is a fine Balance that we must reach in order to achieve it.

Being confident without being vain
Being Undefeatable without being oppressive
Forgiving without being arrogant
Listening without being judgmental
Discernment without paralysis
Giving without expectation
Reconciliation without punishment
Having things without them having us
Having Balance and Power without feeling superior

The answer is a resounding *Yes!!!*

Perhaps it would be nice if there was some great "Deus ex maquina", some supernatural event that could simply breathe this transformation into us.

But we would then not have the benefit of the special journey, effort, challenges, adversity and the satisfaction of attaining growth each of us must experience to attain this transformation to becoming a Powerful Self.

It is in the bit by bit, grinding, grudging, failures, successes, practice and evolving attainment that we reach the ascendance and transcendence that gives the banquet its flavor. It is a worthy and blessed endeavor.

When observing the world around us, it is easy to become confused and troubled by what we see. It seems that globalization has exacerbated the troubles in the world, whether those troubles are pandemics or financial warfare and everything in between. It is a double-edged sword. We want to embrace the whole world, but when the world responds, the repercussions can throw us out of Balance. Capitalism gives, but it also takes. Racial inequality and poverty cry out and demand resolution. The supposed solutions create fear, greed and unconscionable profiteering. The whole of the world seems to be spinning out of control.

From global warming to global cooling. Religious ideologies in a struggle to the death. Politicians of every ilk behaving badly while they line their pockets at the expense of the people. Everyone trying to gain control of everything including our freedoms.

It seems that so many things are broken; and they are. We are all affected in some way. But this is the platform upon which we can launch a new understanding. This is the foundation upon which we can build ourselves into Powerful Beings that the world needs. While all of the world spins wildly, we have this unique opportunity. It is important what happens in the world, both close to us and far away, but when we transcend those troubling events occurring around us, near and far, we become our own Powerful Self. We are unaffected because we release the Darkness from our lives and choose to be at Peace; to live in the Light.

Yes, it is a choice. You may think that your particular crazy life doesn't allow you to make a choice; that your circumstances won't allow it. Think again.

If a soldier who loses both legs in a war can return home from the hospital, his or her life seemingly wrecked and ended forever, and release the darkness, and choose to be happy, have Purpose, be positive and productive; YES!, You too can choose the same.

If Nelson Mandela can be imprisoned for decades in a South African hell hole, and emerge, Undefeatable and rise to leadership of his country against all odds and be at Peace and have Forgiveness, then YES!, You too can choose to live in the Light as he did.

If a father and mother can lose their son to a murderer; suffer their unimaginable pain and loss, yet seek out the parents of the man who killed their son to Reconcile and rebuild all of their lives together; YES!, You too can choose to abandon the Darkness and be transcendent in your life.

If a husband and wife can try to have a child for 15 years, then finally be blessed with the birth of that child, then the child dies in 15 days, yet they try again and re-build their lives and have a child; YES!, You can also be Undefeatable.

Abandon fear; Abandon hatred; Abandon greed. We have been given all of the gifts we need to embrace the Light. Seek these gifts with a sincere spirit. There will always be challenges; there will always be obstacles. That is a part of the journey.

What a sublime knowledge; to know that we can change; to know that transformation is not only possible but that it is already in us and ready to be experienced.

So, what can we, each of us, do to get there? In my experience, I can tell you that it is not an overnight transformation. It is a slow process, occurring one experience at a time; one event at a time. This process is not one of those instant, giddy experiences like one might experience at a rally, a sales convention or religious revival. It is a long-term dedication and commitment to transformation. Take it one step at a time. Place one foot in front of the other, then the next. Be patient. At the end of each day, don't go to sleep until you have reviewed the events of the day and Reconciled any issues, acts, failure to act, events, thoughts, judgments, arguments, comments, arrogant thoughts and any other thing that is on your mind that is keeping you from Peace and Release.

Did I look down on the homeless person standing on the street in front of the office with her shopping cart full of things, all while I was with my fellow workers? Would I have behaved differently if I had been alone? On my way to work in my car, did I honk angrily and shamelessly at the person driving the car ahead of me because they were driving slowly and haltingly? Then when I passed them, I saw an elderly woman who could have been my mother or grandmother, yet I treated them without kindness or consideration. How would I feel if someone treated my mother or grandmother that way?

When my boss berated me for coming in late to work one too many times, did I become defensive and offended and think "she just doesn't understand my life," and then shut down? Should I have instead been thoughtful about what causes my tardiness and offer a constructive solution? How would I feel if I was the boss? Can you change your behavior to respect your employer's time and money?

Did I help my friend in need today and secretly think, "I'll get my reward?" Or should I have helped without thinking of a future reward?

Did I belittle a fellow employee? Did I complain incessantly about my problems? How can I do better?

This daily exercise is a necessary step in helping you Reconcile each day and developing your Powerful Self. Another enjoyable and rewarding exercise is to write. Put into handwritten words your Reconciliations and other thoughts. It's old fashioned much like a diary, but it's an effective exercise and elicits introspection and Truth.

Keep a journal. It's a good friend. You will be very surprised by what you write, but once you get comfortable you will treasure the Liberation, Release and Peace that comes with it. This is the ultimate endeavor. To pursue a God like experience while in a physical existence. To elevate ourselves to the metaphysical and spiritual despite, and perhaps because of, our earthly bondage.

This is our calling. This is our obligation. This is why we are here. I believe that we are at a crucial moment in human existence. A tipping point if you will. I believe that we are at a tipping point of either embracing Darkness or embracing Enlightenment. In this cycle of human evolution, we have a singular window through which to pass. Each of us can influence the final outcome. Each of us will influence the final outcome in one way or another. Which path shall we choose? Whichever path you choose, have no regrets.

"Of all sad words of tongue or pen, the saddest are these,
'It might have been'"

The Beginning

Additional Readings

THE TOUCH OF THE MASTER'S HAND

Twas battered and scarred, and the auctioneer thought it scarcely
worth his while to waste much time on the old violin, but held it up
with a smile;
"what am I bidden, good folks", he cried,
"who will start the bidding for me?"
A dollar, a dollar, then two!!! Only two? Two dollars, and who'll
make it three?? Three dollars, once; three dollars twice; going for
three
But no, from the room, far back, a gray-haired man came forward
and picked up the bow; then wiping the dust from the old violin,
and tightening the loose strings, he played a melody pure and sweet
as a caroling angel sings.
The music ceased, and the auctioneer, with a voice that was quiet
and low, said "what am I bid for the old violin?" And he held it up
with the bow.
"a thousand dollars, and who'll make it two?" Two thousand, and
who'll make it three?" Three thousand once; three thousand twice,
and going and gone!!", said he.
The people cheered, but some of them cried, "we do not quite
understand what changed its worth"
Swift came the reply;
"the touch of the Master's Hand"
And many a man with life out of tune and battered and scarred with
sin, is auctioned cheap to the thoughtless crowd, much like the old
violin. A mess of pottage; a glass of wine; a game, and he travels on.
He is "going once; going twice; he's going and almost gone."
But the Master comes, and the foolish crowd never can quite
understand the worth of a soul and the change that's wrought by
The Touch of the Master's Hand

Myra "Brooks" Welch

Black Elk Speaks

Then I was standing on the highest

Mountain of them all,

Then round about me

Was the whole hoop of the world....

And while I stood there,

I saw more than I could tell,

And I understood more than I saw,

For I was seeing in a sacred manner

The shapes of all things in the spirit,

and the shape of all shapes

As they must live together

Like one being

Black Elk

Invictus

Out of the night that covers me,

Black as the pit from pole to pole,

I thank whatever gods may be

For my unconquerable soul.

In the fell clutch of circumstance

I have not winced nor cried aloud.

Under the bludgeonings of chance

My head is bloody, but unbowed.

Beyond this place of wrath and tears

Looms but the Horror of the shade,

And yet the menace of the years

Finds and shall find me unafraid.

It matters not how strait the gate,

How charged with punishments the scroll,

I am the master of my fate:

I am the captain of my soul.

William Ernest Henley

A PSALM OF LIFE

Tell me not, in mournful numbers,

Life is but an empty dream!

For the soul is dead that slumbers,

And things are not what they seem.

Life is real! Life is earnest!

And the grave is not its goal;

Dust thou art, to dust returnest,

Was not spoken of the soul.

Not enjoyment, and not sorrow,

Is our destined end or way;

But to act, that each to-morrow

Find us farther than to-day.

Art is long, and Time is fleeting,

And our hearts, though stout and brave,

Still, like muffled drums, are beating

Funeral marches to the grave.

In the world's broad field of battle,

In the bivouac of Life,

Be not like dumb, driven cattle!

Be a hero in the strife!

Trust no Future, howe'er pleasant!

Let the dead Past bury its dead!

Act,—act in the living Present!

Heart within, and God o'erhead!

Lives of great men all remind us

We can make our lives sublime,

And, departing, leave behind us

Footprints on the sands of time;

Footprints, that perhaps another,

Sailing o'er life's solemn main,

A forlorn and shipwrecked brother,

Seeing, shall take heart again.

Let us, then, be up and doing,

With a heart for any fate;

Still achieving, still pursuing,

Learn to labor and to wait.

Henry Wadsworth Longfellow

IF

If you can keep your head when all about you
are losing theirs, and blaming it on you;
If you can trust yourself when all men doubt you,
but make allowance for their doubting too;

If you can wait and not be tired by waiting,
Or being lied about, don't deal in lies,
Or being hated, don't give way to hating,
and yet, don't look too good or too wise:

If you can dream-and not make dreams your master;
If you can think-and not make thoughts your aim;
If you can meet with triumph and disaster and treat
those two imposters just the same;

If you can bear to hear the truth you've spoken twisted by
knaves to make a trap for fools, or watch the things you
gave your life to, broken, and stoop and build them up
with worn out tools:

If you can make one heap of all your winnings and risk
it all on one turn of pitch-and-toss, and lose, and start
again at your beginnings and never breathe a word about
your loss;

If you can force your heart and nerve and sinew to serve your
turn long after they are gone, and so hold on when there is
nothing in you except the WILL which says to them: HOLD ON!

If you can talk with crowds and keep your virtue, or walk with
kings, nor lose the common touch;
If all men count with you, but none too much;

If you can fill the unforgiving minute with sixty seconds worth
of distance run, yours is the earth and everything that's in it,
and-which is more, you'll be a man, my son!

Rudyard Kipling

BALANCE

YOU CANNOT BRING ABOUT PROSPERITY

BY DISCOURAGING THRIFT;

YOU CANNOT STRENGTHEN THE WEAK

BY WEAKENING THE STRONG;

YOU CANNOT HELP THE WAGE EARNER

BY PULLING DOWN THE WAGE PAYER;

YOU CANNOT FURTHER THE

BROTHERHOOD OF MAN

BY ENCOURAGING

CLASS HATRED;

YOU CANNOT KEEP OUT OF TROUBLE

BY SPENDING MORE THAN YOU EARN;

YOU CANNOT BUILD

CHARACTER AND COURAGE

BY TAKING AWAY MAN'S

INITIATIVE AND INDEPENDENCE;

YOU CANNOT HELP MEN

PERMANENTLY,

BY DOING FOR THEM

WHAT THEY COULD,

AND SHOULD,

DO FOR THEMSELVES

Atributed to - Abraham Lincoln

AFTERWORD

Afterword

Thank you for joining me in these writings and reflections. They are very personal and I am pleased to have shared them with you. If you have a comment or questions, please email me at: vincent@luzimen.com

The word Luzimen is a word I coined. It means "Light of Mind". Everything I write (other than trivia), is written with the Light of Eternal Mind in my thoughts.

My prior book is called "Entheos, God Within". It is a collection of introspective thoughts, writings, poems and other messages. It is available on Amazon.

I also print Wisdoms on papyrus and frame them. Visit my website @ www.wisdomsbyvincent.com

I wish to thank Donald Ali Roberts for their kind assistance in preparing this book for publication. The immensely interesting art, sketches and drawings on the covers and in this book are their work and their eternal contribution to this combined effort to share Goodness, Purpose, Balance and Power. They have been a joy to work with. You may not believe this, but this is their first time working on a book publication.

We hope to collaborate again on other works.

With much gratitude,

Vincent

About the Author

Vincent was born in the pastoral village of Tome, New Mexico, a village 25 miles south of Albuquerque, New Mexico. His Spanish ancestors settled in the area in the early 1600's and were among the first settlers in Albuquerque's Old Town where he was raised. Brought up in the old ways of hard physical labor, he and his brothers made adobe bricks alongside their father through the summer months starting work at 4am and working until 8pm Monday through Saturday. The rest of the year was busy with Catholic school training under the tutelage of the Sisters of Charity and Jesuit priests, more hard labor after school and rising at 5:30 every morning to ring the old fashioned church bell to call people to Mass at 6am every morning where he served as an altar boy.

In business for himself since the age of 18, Vincent has been involved in business ventures as diverse as real estate development, commercial finance, acquisitions and divestitures, translations and negotiating settlements for adverse parties. He is widely considered a highly skilled negotiator who utilizes the finely honed art and science of inquiry and listening to reach settlements.

It was a decision regarding a loan transaction that resulted in a two year federal prison sentence for which he accepted full responsibility.

Vincent has mentored hundreds of people from a personal growth perspective and in business. He continues to mentor today and mentored several people while in prison.

His forthcoming books include:
Becoming The Total Being
Free Will and Determinism. Confluence or Conflict?
Negotiating from Compassion.
If you would like to ask Vincent a question or contribute to his blog, such as your idea or interpretation of a particular writing, please do so at
vincent@lightofmind.us

About the Artist

D'Ali (they,them) was born and raised in Albuquerque New Mexico. As a nonbinary-African American artist, their influences have been many and their experiences filtered through a unique lens. Nature and emotion fuel D'Ali's artistic works as they play with perception through line, plane, and volume; seeking to develop a visual language in each space.

Currently a masters student enrolled in the School of Architecture and Planning at UNM, D'Ali applies design thinking to many of thier creative processes while allowing art to influence the product as well. This middle space or liminal zone is where they find inspiration. Outside of their academic prospects; D'Ali also is an avid photographer and active in the Arts community of Albuquerque.

D'Ali is available to be reached through their website Donaldaliroberts.com or by email at Daliphoto97@gmail.com

You can find their photography through instagram @darknessabides
You can find their illustrations through instagram @lines_with_feelings_

Reviews

This is a powerful message that everyone who is seeking Balance and Inner Power must read and practice. Vincent's message and delivery are complex but motivating. His message can transform your life and take you from darkness and doubt to Living in Light. I highly recommend this writing for you if you feel lost in this frenzied world.

-DB

I have known the author personally for over 40 years. I can attest that his words are not merely a concatenation of vowels, consonants, verbs and nouns, but a profound and transcendent call to transformation in your life and the peace it can bring to you. Read this message and live it. It will create a metamorphosis in you, and you will never be the same person. Read this message and share it with others. Like knowledge and love, it does not divide, it only multiplies. Read this message. It contemplates your existence in this Eterniverse and beyond.

-PT

The author has written a self-help and inspirational gem sprinkled with applicable anecdotes from his life experiences, including his personal journey to acknowledge and grow from his own misjudgments. He uses this newfound wisdom to encourage the reader to embark on a voyage through self-awareness and enlightenment to a more enriched and less materialistic life. A must-read for those flirting with self-doubt and seeking a spiritual revival.

-Pete David, Author of Mother Nature's Son, L.A. Confrontational, and Second Chance

An Extremely powerful book! The Author, Vincent Garcia, gifts us with deep thoughts and situations we can relate to. He presents us with ways to be engaged in our lives and find balance. Chapter 10, Be Undefeatable, has been my favorite chapter so far, Vincent talks about the power of the mind and how it can hold us back or catapult us forward to success.
"He said he could never scale that wall, and the truth is, he was the only one gaurding it." This and so many other inspiring thoughts make this book a must read. You have to get this book!

Thank you Vincent Garcia. I loved it!!

-Jo-Ann Mascareña

This is a very special and meaningful book! The author is extremely talented in his humble and sincere manner in sharing with us the truth about his life. I am honored to have read his book and provide a commentary and review. Chapter one is my favorite... "Your Book of Life." It includes the phrase, "there is no such things as a normal life, there's just life." (Vida Loca) means crazy life. You are not alone. Everyone has a crazy life whether rich or poor, educated or not. Every chapter in this book has the power to change the life of a human being. After reading it, I choose to see the light and live in the light instead of the darkness. You have to get this book. It can change your life. I love your mind, thoughts and written words.

Thank you Vincent, for sharing them with the world.

M. Sabado